The Process of Biblical Heart Change

by

Julie Ganschow

MABC, Certified Biblical Counselor

and

Bruce Roeder

MA, Certified Biblical Counselor

The Bible versions chosen for inclusion in this book are not intended as an endorsement of any particular version but rather for ease of reading. For in-depth study, the author recommends a more literal version, such as the New American Standard Bible or English Standard Version.

All "counselee" representations are fictitious and do not represent any one person living or dead or their actual case histories or personal stories.

THE PROCESS OF BIBLICAL HEART CHANGE

Copyright © 2013
Published by Pure Water Press, Kansas City, Missouri
Web: www.rgcconline.org
Web: www.biblicalcounselingforwomen.org
Blog: bc4women.org
Email : reigninggracecounsel@rgcconline.org

Cover photography and design by Andrea Loy
www.andrealoydesigns.com

Printed in the United States of America.

Contents

Acknowledgments and Dedication

Acknowledgments:

All projects of this size require many hands to bear good fruit. God has blessed us with a few amazing people that we would like to acknowledge and thank for their valuable help and input into this training manual.

We acknowledge every counselee that has read and taken the little heart change book to heart and experienced a change of life. You were our inspiration to expand it to a training manual.

Mrs. Gaila Roper, our friend and colleague, created a homework piece for the original heart change booklet, and she was our motivation to include questions in the manual. Her firm understanding of that original booklet has been a blessing to many women.

Mrs. Liz Roeder patiently read, edited and re-edited our new material. We thank you Liz for your work for the Lord.

Ms. Jody Lokken patiently flowed the text into the program night after night after working a full day at her "real job." We greatly appreciate your creative insights and dedication to this project and to our ministry.

Ms. Emily Duffey painstakingly edited the text and found all our dangling citations. We are very grateful for the help of these wonderful women.

Dedication:

In the counseling room, nothing is more important than imparting to the counselee the necessity of heart change. In our ministry we have often desired to have the printed word to hand our counselees to reinforce the content of the counseling session regarding the process of mind renewal. What you hold in your hand is the result of this desire. This began as a small booklet that Julie used to speak to her own son about the process of biblical change in his own life. God has since seen fit to use it all over the world and to allow us to expand it into this training manual.

We dedicate this manual to the students of Reigning Grace Counseling Center, past and present. May it be used for the glory of the living God.

Preface

"We have met the enemy and he is us."

This line was uttered by a character that lived in a comic strip swamp who goes by the name of Pogo. Pogo's gloomy, yet accurate insight into the nature of man's heart is sound theology, especially for a comic strip.[1]

Jim Owen, professor of History at the MASTER'S COLLEGE and biblical counselor in the areas of substance abuse and juvenile offenders in California, comments on the prevailing view within today's contemporary evangelical church.

> "Perhaps in this up-beat age of positive thinking and self esteem, we squirm and fret at such a gloomy assessment of ourselves. However, would any of us deny that we have a more than nodding acquaintance with Pogo's wisdom?"[2]

Owen, in my view, is right. We have come a long way from the biblical theology of Augustine, Zwingli, Calvin, Edwards and others who knew what the Scriptures taught about man's heart. Even the fictional character Pogo recognized what the Bible taught about man's sin nature.

John Bunyan, the Reformed Baptist pastor known for writing Pilgrim's Progress, wrote in the 1680s:

> "Sin and corruption would bubble out of my heart as naturally as water bubbles out of a fountain."

Today, if a person like Bunyan would utter words like this, he would at best be diagnosed with some sort of self-esteem problem, and at worst some sort of mental illness or disorder.

Our psychologized view of self, which minimizes or eliminates our sin nature and teaches us we are basically good people, has a direct bearing on how we change, or biblically speaking, how we are sanctified.

If we believe we are basically good people with "good hearts" who sometimes make mistakes, we'll look for some kind of psychological make-over to help us cope with our problems rather than deal with the real issues of the soul. Our misunderstanding of what the heart is leads us away from biblical solutions to the problems that have afflicted man since the Garden of Eden.

Owen comments:

> "The centrality of the Christ and His cross is being replaced by a preoccupation with ourselves - our happiness, our problems, our rights and our worth. Both the uniqueness of the gospel and its integrity are being compromised.

Such a state of compromise has led many Christians into lives filled with desperation and shame, self-abuse and endless guilt, sinful habits and bondage to lust. For many professing Christians there is no new creation, no victory, no joy, no praise. Why not? Because there is no reality of the living Christ, whose grace is more than sufficient."[3]

And it's all because our theology of the heart has been replaced by a non-biblical psychology with an emphasis on feelings and self-worth.

This book is designed to be about biblical change from the heart, and it takes seriously Jesus' teaching about the heart:

> *For there is no good tree which produces bad fruit, nor, on the other hand, a bad tree which produces good fruit. For each tree is known by its own fruit. For men do not gather figs from thorns, nor do they pick grapes from a briar bush. The good man out of the good treasure of his heart brings forth what is good; and the evil man out of the evil treasure brings forth what is evil; for his mouth speaks from that which fills his heart.*
> **Luke 6:43-45 (NASB)**

The core of this book is based on Mrs. Julie Ganschow's booklet titled, THE PROCESS OF BIBLICAL CHANGE.

I've written the introductory chapters regarding the theology of the heart while Mrs. Ganschow has written the chapters on heart change itself, and we have cooperated in the chapters regarding the application of heart change to specific life dominating problems.

This book is designed for use in small groups or as a workbook for individuals. It is also very useful in helping a person understand the core essentials of true biblical counseling. We pray it will be a blessing to you!

Pastor Bruce Roeder

Letter to Students

Dear Beloved Counselee / Student,

Many come looking for counsel because of a problem in their lives. They may have a marriage that is in distress, an eating disorder, sinful anger, depression, anxiety, feelings of being unhappy. Maybe they have relationship problems, drug or alcohol abuse, a struggle with immorality, or a host of other possibilities. Perhaps they have had previous counseling for this same issue. They may have come with a basket of issues that they would like to resolve or gain control of. Most people come for counseling expecting to deal with one or two specific things.

They come with the thought (expectation?) that they will talk about the problem, the counselor will listen and this will somehow make things better in their lives. This has not proven to be an effective method of bringing about real and lasting change.

As a counselor or counselee, what you are about to embark on here is a process. It is the process of biblical change. This change began at your salvation (assuming you know Jesus Christ as your Savior) and will continue until you die when you will be made perfect in all respects. It is a process of leaving behind who you were (Philippians 3:12-14), and revealing Christ in you, the hope of glory. Because it is a process geared toward change, there will be work involved, some practical homework and much more internal working.

My prayer for you is that you grasp the vital importance of biblical change and begin to live your life for the purpose of glorifying God.

> *You were taught, with regard to your former way of life, to put off your old self, which is being corrupted by its deceitful desires; to be made new in the attitude of your minds; and to put on the new self, created to be like God in true righteousness and holiness.*
> **Ephesians 4:22-24 (NIV)**

Julie Ganschow

Section I

Understanding the Basics

Chapter One

Understanding that Heart means Soul

> You must keep all earthly treasures out of your heart, and let Christ be your treasure, and let Him have your heart.
> **C.H. Spurgeon**

Culturally when we speak of the heart, we link it almost exclusively to our emotional component. A phrase like, "speak from the heart" means to say something about how you feel. A phrase like, "follow your heart" means follow your feelings. We live in a culture that is dominated by emotions or feelings. When the heart is not being referred to as the physical organ, it usually means "feelings."

However, the term heart in the Scriptures is rarely used to simply refer to our emotional component. Psalm 73:7 is one such exception:

> *"Their eye bulges from fatness; The imaginations of their heart run riot."* **Psalm 73:7 (NASB)**

Imaginations of the heart means "desires" of the heart. What they want or desire in their hearts (emotions) is running riot. The picture being painted here speaks of being carried away by emotional lusts/wants of the heart. The passage is not an endorsement for anyone to follow their heart (emotions). Actually, it is quite the contrary.

The fact is, the word "heart" in Scripture is usually used in a more comprehensive way than we tend to use the term today.

Question(s) for the reader:
Many people today are what biblical counselors called "psychologized." This means they tend to live their lives dominated by emotions and the therapies designed to help them cope. Their goal in counseling is to "feel better," seeking liberation from negative feelings. All of us are from time to time dominated by emotions, but it may be useful for you to write down the kind of circumstances that tend to evoke dominating negative emotional responses such as fear, worry, anxiety, anger and discouragement.

The Trichotomous View of Man

This point may seem minor until we understand that theology (the study of God) has consequences.

For example, the prevailing view in the evangelical church is that man is a three-part being. The parts are: (1) the physical, (2) the soul, and (3) the spirit. This view is called the trichotomous view of man.

According to the trichotomous view, the physical is the dust of the earth - tissue, bone, muscle, skin, etc. The soul is the inside of man or the immaterial part of man, as is the spirit. The soul, however, is the part of man where emotions reside as well as thoughts. So in this view, man is one part physical and two parts immaterial. This view came to be accepted in evangelical Christianity due to the influence of psychology rather than through the sound exegesis of Scripture.

Winston Smith, biblical counselor for the CHRISTIAN COUNSELING AND EDUCATION CENTER (http://ccef.org) in Pennsylvania, explains what is called the trichotomous view of man:

> Trichotomy is the belief that human beings consist of three components: body, soul, and spirit. While the operations of these three components appear seamless, they are nevertheless distinct and have their discrete properties. Each component, therefore, is considered responsible for overlapping but largely separate operations within human beings: the body for the physical, the soul for the psychological, and the spirit for the spiritual (defined as vertical dimension, relationship with God).[1]

The consequences of this theological thinking are: if you are physically sick you should see a doctor; if you are soul sick you should see a psychologist; and if your spirit is weak you should see a minister. With the plethora of mental illnesses and emotional problems the psychologist has become the soul physician, replacing the minister and Scripture.

Question(s) for the reader:

Have you ever had secular counseling?

Have you ever had counseling that was Christian, but based on the trichotomous view of man?

Do you now see how psychology has come to dominate the church? Can you list examples from your own experience?

Scripture Supports a Dichotomous View

But is man a three-part creature? The scriptural evidence seems to argue for a two-part view.

The Hebrew word for soul is *nephesh* (neh'-fesh). In the New American Standard the term is used 271 times. Psalm 19:7a is a good example:

> *"The word of the Lord is perfect, restoring the soul."*
> **Psalm 19:7a (NASB)**

The word soul in the Old Testament is used to mean living person. For example, in Genesis 2:7 God breathes life into Adam and makes him a living person. The term soul would be inclusive of all the immaterial parts of man including the spirit since Genesis makes no distinction between soul and spirit.

In the New Testament the Greek word for soul is *psyche*, from which we get our modern word, psychiatry.

Strong's defines psyche or soul like this:

> • the seat of the feelings, desires, affections, aversions (our heart, soul, etc.)
> • the soul as an essence that differs from the body and is not dissolved by death (distinguished from other parts of the body)[2]

The biblical definition of this key term says the soul is the seat of feelings (and other things) and not distinct from the spirit. Strong's definition supports the two-part distinction of material/organic and immaterial/inorganic as well as identifying the heart as one and the same thing as the soul.

Scriptural Evidence for the Dichotomous View

But you might say, could Strong's be wrong? Certainly there must be scriptural evidence to support the three-part view of body, soul, and spirit or Christians would not hold to it. Christians who take the three-part view do so by misinterpreting some biblical texts that at first glance seem to make a distinction between the physical, spirit, and soul. Hebrews 4:12 is the best case in point.

> *For the word of God is living and powerful, and sharper than any two-edged sword, piercing even to the division of soul and spirit, and of joints and marrow, and is a discerner of the thoughts and intents of the heart.*
> **Hebrews 4:12 (NKJV)**

17

Here we see soul and spirit used in the same sentence as if they are two separate things. The word division seems to make the point.

Dr. Jay E. Adams comments:

> Let us first consider Hebrews 4:12. There, we are told, "God's Word, the Bible, is likened to a sharp, flashing two-edged sword that is able to penetrate deeply enough to divide between soul and spirit, just as it can divide between joints and marrow." "See" say those who advocate triplexity, "if the Scriptures affirm the possibility of dividing soul from spirit, so should we." But the fact is that the Greek doesn't do any such thing. The KJV (and some subsequent translations) mislead the English reader. The point is not that the soul is divided from the spirit, or joint from marrow. Rather, what is said is that God's word splits the spirit and also the soul, the joints and also the marrow.... The true idea is that God's Word penetrates deeply enough into man's innermost being to cut open and lay bare his desires and thoughts.[3]

Dr. John MacArthur comments on soul and spirit in Hebrews 4:12:

> These terms do not describe two separate entities (any more than "thoughts and intents" do), but are used as one might say "heart and soul" to express. Elsewhere these two terms are used interchangeably to describe man's immaterial self, his eternal inner person.[4]

Luke 10:27 supports Dr. MacArthur's and Dr. Adams' analysis.

As Jesus makes the point of the first great commandment, He is not making a distinction between soul and heart, and strength and mind. He is saying to love the Lord your God with all you are.

> *So he answered and said, you shall love the Lord your God with all your heart, with all your soul, with all your strength, and with all your mind, and your neighbor as yourself.*
> **Luke 10:47**

By looking at other Scriptures we can deduce with a high level of accuracy that in Hebrews 4:12 spirit and soul mean the same thing and are not two separate parts.

The writer is emphasizing the power of God's Word and what it accomplishes in the human heart. He is not writing to convince anyone that soul and spirit are different.

> As we prayerfully expose ourselves to the Scriptures, we begin to understand what God's will is regarding our conduct and character. And then as the Holy Spirit applies His word to specific areas of our lives, and as we are obedient to His promptings, we begin to develop Bible-based convictions. Our values begin to change so that God's standard becomes our delight and our desire.[5]
>
> **Jerry Bridges**

Another passage that at first glance seems to make a distinction between soul and spirit is 1 Thessalonians 5:23:

The key in understanding this passage is to understand what Paul is saying by the word completely - to be sanctified thoroughly. "Completely" is a comprehensive reference amplified by "your whole spirit, soul, and body." He is not arguing for three separate parts of man, but using synonyms to drive home his point. Again, it would seem that fullness is the emphasis.

> *Now may the God of peace Himself sanctify you completely; and may your whole spirit, soul, and body be preserved blameless at the coming of our Lord Jesus Christ.*
>
> **I Thessalonians 5:23**

Dr. MacArthur:

> This comprehensive reference makes the term "completely" more emphatic. By using spirit and soul, Paul was not indicating that the immaterial part of man could be divided into two substances (cf. Heb. 4:12). The two words are used interchangeably throughout Scripture (cf. Heb. 6:19; 10:39; 1 Pet. 2:11; 2 Pet. 2:8). There can be no division of these realities, but rather they are used as other texts use multiple terms for emphasis (cf. Deut. 6:5; Matt. 22:37; Mark 12:30; Luke 10:27). Nor was Paul a believer in a three-part human composition (cf. Rom. 8:10; 1 Cor. 2:11; 5:3–5; 7:34; 2 Cor. 7:1; Gal. 6:18; Col. 2:5; 2 Tim. 4:22), but rather two parts: material and immaterial.[6]

In fact, the two words of soul and spirit are used interchangeably throughout Scripture; nowhere does Paul argue for a three-part composition of man. However, the consequences of accepting a three-part view of man are devastating. Winston Smith again writes:

> Divorced from a truly biblical understanding of the heart as the seat of human motivations and behavior, the gospel and the commands of God are superficial and ineffective, only vaguely relevant to "psychological problems," and irrelevant to "physiological problems."[7]

This is why it is important to have a biblical theology of the soul and not a theology of the soul as seen through the lens of psychology.

Inner Man, Outer Man

As will be noted later, the Bible makes a distinction between the "outer man" and the "inner man," or as Dr. Adams puts it, a duplex view of man that emphasizes the unity of the elements (meaning they are folded together rather than their separability).[8]

The inner man refers to the thoughts, desires, will, and emotions, as well as his spirit. The outer man is the physical—that part of man that is subject to decay (2 Cor. 4:16).

> *Therefore, we do not lose heart, but though our outer man is decaying, yet our inner man is being renewed day by day.*
> **2 Corinthians 4:16 (NASB)**

All the aspects of the inner man are captured by the word "heart." Thayer's Greek Dictionary defines heart like this:

Kardia: the soul or mind, as it is the fountain and seat of the thoughts, passions, desires, appetites, affections, purposes, endeavors of the will and character of the soul so far as it is affected and stirred in a bad way or good, or of the soul as the seat of the sensibilities, affections, emotions, desires, appetites, passions.[9]

From these considerations we can clearly see that the heart and soul are one and the same thing, and by no means is the word "heart" confined to mean "how we feel." What makes matters worse is that when we trust our feelings in order to make decisions or "speak truth to us" we often rationalize sin. For example, how many Christian divorces have taken place because the feeling of love is not what it used to be? How many Christians equate feelings of sadness with, "I must be sick or have some sort of depression disorder?" How many people make decisions based on the fuzziness of "following your heart?"

For example, as a biblical counselor I have had people tell me they have made a certain decision because they prayed about it and "had a peace in their heart." This is the Christian version of following your heart. A couple of examples I've seen are starting a business that failed or making a move that bordered on the irrational.

The language reflects a subjective, experiential, feelings-approach to life rather than a solid, scriptural approach to life.

In space, astronauts experience the misery of having no reference point, no force that draws them to the center. Where there is no "moral gravity"- that is, no force that draws us to the center- there is spiritual weightlessness. We float on feelings that will carry us where we were never meant to go; we bubble with emotional experiences that we often take for spiritual ones; and we are puffed up with pride. Instead of seriousness, there is foolishness. Instead of gravity, flippancy. Sentimentality takes the place of theology. Our reference point will never serve to keep our feet on solid rock. Our reference point, until we answer God's call, is merely ourselves. We cannot possibly tell which end is up.[10]   **Elisabeth Elliot**

Question(s) for the reader:

Have you ever used this type of feelings-oriented language yourself? In what way?

Can you think of a time when you have been counseled to "follow your heart?" What was the particular issue?

Did you follow the counsel and what was the outcome?

After reading through this material, how has your view of the heart changed? Or hasn't it? Why or why not?

A biblical understanding of the heart is necessary before we can understand how to change to glorify God. But we also need to understand our true heart's condition so that we see our desperate need for a Savior and His righteousness.

Chapter Two

Understanding the Fall

It is very popular today in many churches to say that man (and his soul) is basically good. The notion that man is basically good is perpetrated in the church by a psychologized gospel that exalts man.

> "Self" is at the center of our lusts—our supposed needs for significance, worth, security, identity, or esteem. A psychologized, man-centered view of God and of man appeals to our natural sense of loving ourselves and thus deceives us.[1]
> **Martha Peace**

Is Man Basically Good?

One popular poll asked professing evangelicals if man was basically good or bad. The astounding results showed that 77% believed man was basically good. Perhaps we should not be surprised by this as many preachers are preaching messages that are based on making people "feel good" about themselves.

> It is no secret that Christ's Church is not in good health in many places of the world. She has been languishing because she has been fed, as the current line has it, 'junk food;' all kinds of artificial preservatives and all sorts of unnatural substitutes have been served up to her. As a result, theological and biblical malnutrition has afflicted the very generation that has taken such giant steps to make sure its physical health is not damaged by using foods or products that are harmful to their bodies. Simultaneously a worldwide spiritual famine resulting from the absence of any genuine publication of the Word of God (Amos 8:11) continues to run wild and almost unabated in most quarters of the Church.[2]   **Walter Kaiser**

Man was created by God in His image. The Scripture teaches that man was created sin-free and has a rational nature, intelligence, will, and moral responsibility (Gen. 1:26-28). But being created in the image of God does not mean that man is basically good by nature.

Adam and Eve disobeyed God and lost their innocence (Rom. 5:12). Man was guilty of sin and incurred the penalty of spiritual and physical death becoming subject to God's wrath because God cannot tolerate sin. Man then became inherently corrupt and totally incapable of choosing or doing that which is acceptable to God apart from divine grace (Rom. 5:19). Man, thereby, has no power

within himself to recover and is hopelessly lost. Historically, this radical corruption of the soul has been called "total inability." Wayne Grudem explains:

> In Our Natures We Totally Lack Spiritual Good Before God: It is not just that some parts of us are sinful and others are pure. Rather, every part of our being is affected by sin—our intellects, our emotions and desires, our hearts (the center of our desires and decision-making processes), our goals and motives, and even our physical bodies. Paul says, *"I know that nothing good dwells within me, that is, in my flesh"* (Rom. 7:18) and, *"to the corrupt and unbelieving nothing is pure; their very minds and consciences are corrupted"* (Titus 1:15). Moreover, Jeremiah tells us that *"the heart is deceitful above all things, and desperately corrupt; who can understand it?"* (Jer. 17:9). In these passages Scripture is not denying that unbelievers can do good in human society in some sense. But it is denying that they can do any spiritual good or be good in terms of a relationship with God. Apart from the work of Christ in our lives, we are like all other unbelievers who are *"darkened in their understanding, alienated from the life of God because of the ignorance that is in them, due to their hardness of heart."* Ephesians 4:18 (ESV)[3]

Grudem notes that total inability does not mean that every person is as bad as he or she might be, for God's common grace restrains unredeemed sinners from fully realizing their sinful potential. Every person has the potential for even the worst of sins, since every aspect of a person was affected by the fall (will, emotions, thoughts, etc.). Scripture (see Romans 12:16) indicates we are inclined to think too highly of ourselves and our "goodness." We are more prideful than we want to believe!

Question(s) for the reader:

What have you been taught over the years? Is man basically good or basically bad? What Scriptures would you cite to support your answer?

Note the condition of the unredeemed heart in these Scriptures:

The True Condition of the Heart

Then the LORD saw that the wickedness of man was great on the earth, and that every intent of the thoughts of his heart was only evil continually. **Genesis 6:5 (NASB)**

This is one of the strongest and clearest statements about man's sinful nature. The people of Noah's day were exceedingly wicked from the inside out. Why? Because the fall affected every aspect of the heart.

> There is a dark truth about man. Because of this truth he can never with credibility claim, 'I did not mean it,' or, 'I didn't know what I was saying,' for the truth is we, in some sense, mean what we say.[4]
> **Howard Eyrich and William Hines**

The heart is deceitful above all things, and desperately wicked; Who can know it? **Jeremiah 17:9 (NKJV)**

The prophet Jeremiah declares the heart is deceitful above all things and desperately wicked. At the very least it means our hearts cannot be trusted. Yet, in our culture we constantly hear from psychology that we are to follow our hearts, make the right heart choice, that your heart can be trusted to guide you.

When these things are said, they are, in fact, equating feelings with the heart. Clearly, that notion is contradicted directly by what God says - do not trust your heart emotions because they are deceitful and cannot be trusted to lead you.

For from within, out of the heart of men, proceed the evil thoughts, fornications, thefts, murders, adulteries, … **Mark 7:21 (NASB)**

Jesus Himself reveals the true condition of men's hearts. The inner man is not "basically good" but seriously flawed and utterly corrupt, and without the grace of God, will remain so. Since Adam all men and women are sinners by nature and by choice, so it would be accurate to describe ourselves as basically depraved and not basically good (See Romans 3:9-18, 23; 5:10-12).

> As the salt flavors every drop in the Atlantic, so does sin affect every atom of our nature. It is so sadly there, so abundantly there, that if you cannot detect it, you are deceived. **C.H. Spurgeon**

Proverbs indicates it is folly to trust in one own's heart:

> *He who trusts in his own heart is a fool, but he who walks wisely will be delivered.*   **Proverbs 28:26 (NASB)**

Instead, we are to trust in the Lord (and His Word), not relying on our hearts.

> *Trust in the Lord with all your heart, and lean not on your own understanding...*   **Proverbs 3:5 (NASB)**

The Heart is Desperately Wicked

We must realize the heart has been affected by the fall. The following diagram illustrates this:

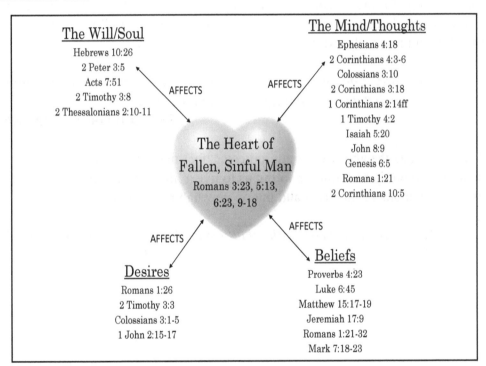

Question(s) for the reader:
What do the following passages indicate about the heart without Christ?
1 Corinthians 1:18

1 Corinthians 2:14

Romans 8:7

Ephesians 4:17-18

Romans 3:9-18

Genuine Hope

> The inability to love, obey, or please God is the very essence of human depravity. And the only solution to that predicament is the re-creative work of God (2 Cor. 5:17). That is why Jesus told Nicodemus, *"You must be born again"* (John 3:7). *"Unless one is born again, he cannot see the kingdom of God"* (John 3:3). This is what salvation is all about: God miraculously changes the nature of those whom He redeems, so that they are drawn to the very same righteousness they formerly hated. This was the central promise of the New Covenant.[5] **John MacArthur**

In the above chart we see just how bad the bad news is, and how our hearts (souls) have been affected. But in realizing just how bad the bad news is, we also recognize there is hope. There is hope for sinful man and his bad heart. There is hope for the person who has truly received Christ as Savior and Lord. The Bible declares that a person who has been "born-again" has a new heart that did not previously exist.

> *Therefore, if any man is in Christ he is a new creature, the old things have passed away; behold, new things have come.*
> **2 Corinthians 5:17 (NASB)**

This means, as the above diagram indicates, that the Holy Spirit will apply redemption to our hearts, thus enabling us to live a life pleasing to Him as we put off our old habits of the heart and put on new habits of the heart.

> *Watch over your heart with all diligence, for from it flow the springs of life.*
> **Proverbs 4:23 (NASB)**

Chapter Three

Understanding Salvation

> Justification is indeed God's answer to the most important of all human questions: How can a man or a woman become right with God? We are not right with God in ourselves. We are under God's wrath. Justification is vital, because we must become right with God or perish eternally... The difficulty is that most people today do not actually feel a need in this area. Martin Luther did; it is what haunted him. He knew he was not right with God, and he anticipated a confrontation with an angry God at the final judgment. God showed him that he could experience a right relationship with God through the work of Jesus Christ. But who feels the intensity of Luther's anguish today?[1]　　**James Boice**

Only God can change the human heart

And I will give you a new heart with new and right desires, and I will put a new spirit in you. I will take out your stony heart of sin and give you a new, obedient heart.　　**Ezekiel 36:26 (NLT)**

And I will give them singleness of heart and put a new spirit within them. I will take away their hearts of stone and give them tender hearts instead, so they will obey My laws and regulations. Then they will truly be My people, and I will be their God.　　**Ezekiel 11:19-20 (NLT)**

And I will give them one heart and mind to worship Me forever, for their own good and for the good of all their descendants.

Jeremiah 32:39 (NLT)

A new heart is given by God at salvation.
Salvation is necessary because of sin.

> O sinner, can you give any reason why, since you have risen from your bed this morning, God has not stricken you dead?　　**Jonathan Edwards**
>
> Christianity insists that everyone is a sinner through and through. Our minds, hearts, wills, and emotions are in rebellion against God. When it comes right down to it, the problem is not that there is only one way to God (through Christ). The real problem is that human beings will not follow God at all.[2]　　**Philip Graham Ryken**

For all have sinned; all fall short of God's glorious standard.
Romans 3:23 (NLT)

Psalm 51 is the account of David, "a man after God's own heart" who sinned greatly in his life. Read his words below:

Have mercy on me, O God, because of your unfailing love. Because of your great compassion, blot out the stain of my sins. Wash me clean from my guilt. Purify me from my sin. For I recognize my shameful deeds— they haunt me day and night. Against you, and you alone, have I sinned; I have done what is evil in your sight. You will be proved right in what you say, and your judgment against me is just. For I was born a sinner—yes, from the moment my mother conceived me. But you desire honesty from the heart, so you can teach me to be wise in my inmost be-ing. Purify me from my sins, and I will be clean; wash me, and I will be whiter than snow. **Psalm 51:1-7 (NLT)**

This wise man recognized that he was in deep trouble. He knew his sin had separated him from God. It wasn't just the sin he committed at that time, but he admits he "was born a sinner." He understands there will be judgment for his sin and he asks for pardon from his sins, for redemption, for salvation.

First Corinthians 6:9-10 tell us that because of all their sin the unsaved will not inherit the kingdom of God.

Do you not know that the wicked will not inherit the kingdom of God? Do not be deceived: Neither the sexually immoral nor idolaters nor adulterers nor male prostitutes nor homosexual offenders nor thieves nor the greedy nor drunkards nor slanderers nor swindlers will inherit the kingdom of God. **1 Corinthians 6:9-10 (NIV)**

But the cowardly, the unbelieving, the vile, the murderers, the sexually immoral, those who practice magic arts, the idolaters and all liars— their place will be in the fiery lake of burning sulfur. This is the second death. **Revelation 21:8 (NIV)**

To not "inherit the kingdom of God" means that you will be eternally separated from Him. When you take your last breath you will be lost and without hope for all eternity. There will be no second chance or reprieve.

Perhaps you have heard this before and discounted it. I would urge you not to harden your heart today.

...But no, you won't listen. So you are storing up terrible punishment for yourself because of your stubbornness in refusing to turn from your sin.

28

For there is going to come a day of judgment when God, the just judge of all the world, will judge all people according to what they have done. He will give eternal life to those who persist in doing what is good, seeking after the glory and honor and immortality that God offers. But he will pour out his anger and wrath on those who live for themselves, who refuse to obey the truth and practice evil deeds. **Romans 2:5-8 (NLT)**

Before we can fully appreciate the good news found in Christ alone, we have to first grasp just how bad the bad news is and realize our desperate lost condition.

> For the wages of sin is death, but the gift of God is eternal life in Christ Jesus our Lord.
> **Romans 6:23 (NIV)**

The good news is that Jesus Christ came to redeem sinners, and to set us free from the penalty of sin and death.

But God showed his great love for us by sending Christ to die for us while we were still sinners. And since we have been made right in God's sight by the blood of Christ, he will certainly save us from God's judgment.

Romans 5:8-9 (NLT)

God has provided a way for you to be made right with Him through Jesus Christ.

For God made Christ, who never sinned, to be the offering for our sin, so that we could be made right with God through Christ.
2 Corinthians 5:21 (NLT)

The only way to be made right with God is through Jesus Christ. It is essential that you understand and believe that there is *nothing* you can do to save yourself.

...the sinful mind is hostile to God. It does not submit to God's law, nor can it do so. Those controlled by the sinful nature cannot please God.
Romans 8:7-8 (NIV)

Without Christ it is impossible to submit to God or obey Him

Once you were dead, doomed forever because of your many sins. You used to live just like the rest of the world, full of sin, obeying Satan, the mighty prince of the power of the air. He is the spirit at work in the hearts of those who refuse to obey God. All of us used to live that way, following the passions and desires of our evil nature. We were born with an evil nature, and we were under God's anger just like everyone else.
Ephesians 2:1-3 (NLT)

*But God is so rich in mercy, and he loved us so very much, that even while we were dead because of our sins, **he gave us life** when he raised Christ from the dead. (It is only by God's special favor [grace]that you have been saved!)* **Ephesians 2:4-5 (NLT)**

*God saved you by his special favor (grace)when you believed. **And you can't take credit for this; it is a gift from God**. Salvation is not a reward for the good things we have done, so none of us can boast about it.* **Ephesians 2:8-9 (NLT)**

*He saved us, **not because of the good things we did**, but because of his mercy. He washed away our sins and gave us a new life through the Holy Spirit. He generously poured out the Spirit upon us because of what Jesus Christ our Savior did. He declared us not guilty (justification) because of his great kindness. And now we know that we will inherit eternal life.* **Titus 3:5-7 (NLT)**

Salvation is a gift of God that we receive by faith. You must believe that you are a sinner in need of salvation, there is no way to save yourself from the penalty of your sin, and believe that Jesus Christ came to pay the penalty for it by giving His life for you on the cross.

Question(s) for the reader:
Have you ever truly been amazed by God's grace?

In this space provide a biblical definition of what grace is. For help with this, Read Romans, Chapters 1-5 and then look up the following Scriptures from Romans, Chapter 5 to help you with the definition. (Romans 5:2,15, 17,20-21)

Look up Romans 8:28-39, study it, and see if you can list ten things that are so amazing about God's grace.

After you finish your study of Romans 5 and 8 write down at least one thing that is troubling you now. Then examine the problem in light of what you learned in your study of God's grace.

For Christ died for sins once for all, the righteous for the unrighteous, to bring you to God. He was put to death in the body but made alive by the Spirit.

1 Peter 3:18 (NIV)

Do you see your need for the Savior?

There is much confusion about how a person gets saved or redeemed due to the influence of evangelistic methods that promote praying a prayer or asking Jesus into your heart.

There is no prayer that saves you. There is no special formula to receive Christ.

What is necessary is a biblical response to the gospel. You must understand that you are a sinner in need of salvation and that you cannot save yourself by any works or deeds. You must believe by faith that Jesus Christ came to be your Savior and that He died on the cross for our sins and accept His free gift of salvation.

You have been divinely enabled to believe and respond to the gospel by God and in that first moment of belief several amazing things take place.

You are justified in Christ. You are adopted as a child of God. You are set apart (sanctified) and made righteous before God. You also gain access to the throne room of God because you are no longer an enemy who is under His wrath, but His beloved child.

He also comes to dwell within you in the person of the Holy Spirit and you are changed forever.

He removes your heart of stone and gives you a heart of flesh that is able to be transformed and conformed to the image and likeness of Christ.

If you want to pray a prayer, there is of course no harm in talking to God about what He has done for you in Christ.

Many people are moved to confession of sin and repentance as a part of what God is supernaturally doing within them. It is critical you understand it is faith—not a prayer—that saves you.

> *For if you confess with your mouth that Jesus is Lord and believe in your heart that God raised him from the dead, you will be saved. For it is by believing in your heart that you are made right with God, and it is by confessing with your mouth that you are saved. As the Scriptures tell us, "Anyone who believes in him will not be disappointed." Jew and Gentile are the same in this respect. They all have the same Lord, who generously gives his riches to all who ask for them. For "Anyone who calls on the name of the Lord will be saved."* **Romans 10:9-13 (NLT)**

> *Therefore, since we have been made right in God's sight by faith, we have peace with God because of what Jesus Christ our Lord has done for us.* **Romans 5:1 (NLT)**

> *...But you were washed, you were sanctified, you were justified in the name of the Lord Jesus Christ and by the Spirit of our God.* **1 Corinthians 6:11 (ESV)**

Even though we have been given a new heart when the Holy Spirit sovereignly regenerates us (Jn. 1:12-13; 3:3-8), we still deal with unconquered sin and the desires of the heart that lead to idolatry. Paul, in the seventh chapter of Romans, identifies our struggle with the flesh.

> *The law is good, then. The trouble is not with the law but with me, because I am sold into slavery, with sin as my master. I don't understand*

myself at all, for I really want to do what is right, but I don't do it. Instead, I do the very thing I hate. I know perfectly well that what I am doing is wrong, and my bad conscience shows that I agree that the law is good. But I can't help myself, because it is sin inside me that makes me do these evil things.

I know I am rotten through and through so far as my old sinful nature is concerned. No matter which way I turn, I can't make myself do right. I want to, but I can't. When I want to do good, I don't. And when I try not to do wrong, I do it anyway. But if I am doing what I don't want to do, I am not really the one doing it; the sin within me is doing it. It seems to be a fact of life that when I want to do what is right, I inevitably do what is wrong. I love God's law with all my heart.

Romans 7:14-22 (NLT)

Salvation in Jesus Christ is what brings the ability for subsequent heart change.

Paul recognizes that his only hope for change is in Jesus Christ.

Oh, what a miserable person I am! Who will free me from this life that is dominated by sin? Thank God! The answer is in Jesus Christ our Lord. So you see how it is: In my mind I really want to obey God's law, but because of my sinful nature I am a slave to sin. **Romans 7:24-25 (NLT)**

Once saved, you have now been enabled to change on the heart level (mind, thoughts, desires, intentions, emotions) through the Person of Christ and the power of the Holy Spirit living His life in you. The Lord empowers you to make the changes in your heart that are evidenced in your behavior.

Question(s) for the reader:
Read Hebrews 11:1. How do you assess your own assurance of your salvation? Do you assess your assurance on the basis of emotions (how you feel), personal experience or on the promises of God?

What do John 5:24, 11:25-26 promise?

What would it mean in your daily life to fully embrace God's plan of redemption?

C.J. Mahaney wrote in *Living The Cross Centered Life*:

> Each of our lives is centered on something. What's the center of yours? Think about it for a moment. What's really the main thing in your life? Only one thing can truly be first in priority; so what's at the top of your list, second to none?
>
> Or let me put it this way: What are you most passionate about? What do you love to talk about? What do you think about most often when your mind is free?
>
> Or try this: What is it that defines you? Is it your career? A relationship? Maybe it's your family, or your ministry. It could be some cause or movement, or some political affiliation. Or perhaps your main thing is a hobby or a talent you have, or even your house and possessions.[3]
>
> **C.J. Mahaney**

It could be one of any number of good things, but when it comes to the center of our life, what really qualifies as the one thing God says should be the most important?

Here's how the apostle Paul would answer the question:

> *Now let me remind you, dear brothers and sisters, of the Good News I preached to you before. You welcomed it then and still do now, for your faith is built on this wonderful message. I passed on to you what was most important and what had also been passed on to me—that Christ died for our sins, just as the Scriptures said.*
>
> **1 Corinthians 15:1, 3 (NLT)**

Repentance

There are many questions regarding repentance and how to know when a person has truly repented of any kind of sin. Repentance is critical in overcoming any kind of sin.

Biblically true repentance is a threefold response to sin that is found in the use of three different words that express a different aspect of repentance. All three components or aspects must be present for there to be fruit of true repentance in a person's life.

The first response of repentance is found in the Greek word metanoeo which means a "change of mind" (Matt. 3:2, Mark 1:15).

When a person has a change of mind it means that there has been acknowledgment of sin. This is what we find when a person confesses their sin. They admit and understand that what they have done is sinful. There is no justification or rationalization attached to the sin, no attempts to minimize or blame shift the responsibility for it onto someone else. There is personal guilt attached to the acts that have been committed.

Repentance cannot stop here because it is incomplete. There are plenty of situations where a person has confessed sin and admitted their guilt and nothing more happens. There is no other visible change and things go back to normal; meaning the sin resumes at some point or something else takes its place.

An excellent example of this would be the Pharaoh as he dealt with Moses and the Israelites. Twice (Ex. 9:27; 10:16) he admitted to Moses, "I have sinned against the Lord your God." He admitted he sinned, he did not justify or rationalize or shift the blame and yet he did not repent. There were no changes that accompanied his admission; in fact, he went right back to his behavior!

King Saul had the same kind of limited repentance (1 Sam. 15:24, 24:17; 26:21) and he did not cease in pursuing David no matter how sorry he was. It is clear that just admitting sin does not equal repentance.

The second critical aspect of repentance is metanolomai (Matt. 21:29, 32; Heb. 7:21) and it means "change of heart." In addition to admitting and confessing sin there must be a change of heart with respect to the sin; what a person once loved and worshiped is now hated.

There is no longer room in the heart for fulfilling various lusts; in fact there is a growing hatred for everything that leads to that particular sin in the first place. We could call this a holy hatred and it is an emotional response that is experienced in the body in the form of deep sorrow over their sin.

Worldly Sorrow/Godly Sorrow

An important difference must be made here: there is a great difference between worldly sorrow and godly sorrow. Godly sorrow has as its first concern the honor of God. It is other's oriented and is produced by the Holy Spirit acting on the conscience of a sinner. This kind of sorrow cries out, "Woe is me" and causes a person to weep bitterly over the sin that has been committed.

When the Apostle Peter denied Christ three times after the arrest of Jesus he went off and wept (metanoeo). He was heartbroken over his sin and over how he had betrayed the One he loved. By comparison Judas also repented (metamelo-mai), meaning he had a change of heart about betraying an innocent man. He felt guilty about it and sought to rectify it by returning the money he was paid and his hope was to erase his guilt and somehow undo what he had done. He then went and hung himself (Matt. 27:3-5).

It is important to note that repentance is a manifestation of the life of Christ in a person. It is a proof of salvation in a person's life. The sinner (Peter in the above example) has been cut deeply to the heart by the Spirit of God and or the Word of God and understands that his sin is grievous to the Lord. Because of accepting and understanding that spiritual reality, he no longer desire to participate in it.

Worldly sorrow is "unsanctified remorse"[i] (Judas in the above example) and is focused on feelings of regret, fear, and even desperation. Its focus is on how the sin or its exposure will affect him. MacArthur further says that worldly sorrow "has no redemptive capability. It is nothing more than the wounded pride of getting caught in a sin and having one's lusts go unfulfilled."[ii]

The first two kinds of repentance take place in the inner man, or the heart. This is critical because as the heart is changed the actions change, which lead us to the third part of this critical aspect of change.

Finally, there must be metanoia which is a "change the course of life" (Matt. 3:8; 9:13; Acts 20:21). We know that the Apostle Peter truly did repent because his life demonstrated all of the aspects of repentance: he understood his sin (fear), he grieved over his sin (fear of man) and his life changed (he boldly proclaimed Christ for the rest of his life, ultimately being martyred for the faith).

Changing the course of life involves an act of the will, a turning from the sinful behavior. There must be a radical amputation of the actions.

"If your hand causes you to stumble, cut it off; it is better for you to enter life crippled, than, having your two hands, to go into hell, into the unquenchable fire,[where their worm does not die, and the fire is not quenched.] "If your foot causes you to stumble, cut it off; it is better for you to enter life lame, than, having your two feet, to be cast into hell, [where their worm does not die, and the fire is not quenched.] "If your eye causes you to stumble, throw it out; it is better for you to enter the kingdom of God with one eye, than, having two eyes, to be cast into hell, Mark 9:43-47

---

[i] John MacArthur Study Bible footnotes on 2 Corinthians 7:10
[ii] Ibid·

When repentance is genuine you will see all of this and the change will be dramatic.

Repentance is not something a person can conjure up from within. No amount of screaming or threatening or other forms of manipulation will force a person to repent. Repentance is a gift from God. Repentance can come quickly or sometimes will take years but one thing is for certain: a regenerated Christian will repent. There will be no way for a person to live under the conviction and ministry of the Holy Spirit without repenting.

Section II

Understanding the Process

Chapter Four

Understanding Your Present Heart Condition

As we approach the process of biblical heart change, we will summarize the material from chapters 1-3 and expound in the area of personal application in chapters 4-6.

What is the "heart"?

Definition: The heart is the biblical word used to describe the inner man. The heart is the immaterial (non-flesh) part of a person that includes our thoughts, beliefs, desires, mind, feelings, intentions, and emotions. It is often referred to as the control center of our being.

We are made of two parts

Material / Immaterial

What we think, believe, and desire in our immaterial part (mind, heart, soul, feelings), is what our material part (body) does. For example, when we think we are thirsty, we get up and get a drink. If we believe we are in danger, we run. If we desire an ice cream cone, we get one. We are used to our bodies automatically responding to these commands.

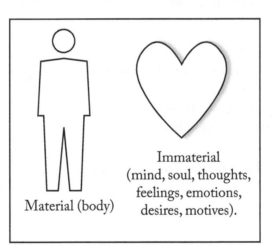

Material (body)

Immaterial (mind, soul, thoughts, feelings, emotions, desires, motives).

We also automatically respond to other kinds of thoughts and desires. When we become angry, we may curse or hit. When we desire escape from problems, we may drink or use drugs. When we want something and don't have the money to purchase it, we may steal or put it on credit. When we are in trouble, we may fear exposure so we lie. These things may have become automatic for you, too.

Through repetition, various actions become a habit or pattern. We refer to these habits as automatic behaviors. They become the default position we assume when angry, sad, upset, or lonely. The basis for these sinful patterns are found in the heart.

41

However, our sinful actions usually do not stem from a failure to achieve but from an inner urge to fulfill our own desires.

This means that we have trained ourselves to respond in certain ways when confronted by a circumstance or situation.

> "Each person is tempted when he is lured and enticed by his own desire."
> **James 1:14 (ESV)**

> We gossip or lust because of the sinful pleasure we get out of it. At that time, the lure of that momentary pleasure is stronger than our desire to please God[1]
> **Jerry Bridges**

For example, for years I (Julie) bit my fingernails when I was nervous or upset. It was something I was not even aware I was doing much of the time. When I was fretting about something, my fingers went right to my mouth, and before I knew it, my fingers were bleeding. Many people have learned to comfort themselves with food when sad or upset. Some who struggle with pornography cite loneliness as their trigger for self-gratification as an automatic behavior.

> The acceptable sins are subtle in the sense that they deceive us into thinking they are not so bad, or not thinking of them as sins, or even worse, not even thinking about them at all! Yes, some of our refined sins are so subtle that we commit them without even thinking about them, either at the time or afterward. We often live in unconscious denial of our 'acceptable' sins.[2]
> **Jerry Bridges**

By the same token, I (Bruce) used to have a job that was very boring. When I would think about going to the job, I would become sad or discouraged and these feelings would sometimes lead to anger. Because I had to go to a job every day I did not like, I had trained myself to see the work through the eyes of boredom.

Question(s) for the reader:
How have you trained yourself to respond to certain situations in your life?

Write out the automatic behaviors you know you struggle with.

The Bible has much to say about the heart

When helping a person in the process of change, the most critical aspect of this is showing a person the importance the heart plays in life and in behavior.

Careful use of the Scriptures will bring the convicting power of the Holy Spirit to bear in a person's life.

> *As in water face reflects face, so a man's heart reveals the man.*
> **Proverbs 27:19 (NKJV)**

What does this mean?

As water acts like a mirror and shows what we look like on the outside, the heart reflects and reveals what we are like on the inside.

> *The good man brings good things out of the good stored up in his heart, and the evil man brings evil things out of the evil stored up in his heart. For out of the overflow of his heart his mouth speaks.* **Luke 6:45 (NIV)**

> *But the things that come out of the mouth come from the heart, and these make a man 'unclean.' For out of the heart come evil thoughts, murder, adultery, sexual immorality, theft, false testimony, slander.*
> **Matthew 15:18-19 (NIV)**

Question(s) for the reader:

What does Proverbs 4:27 say about behavior?

What do Proverbs 15:15, 30 say about feelings?

What does Proverbs 28:14 say about attitudes?

As you look at your own life in comparison with the above passages, examine your actions over the past week. Have you struggled with evil thoughts, bitterness, immorality, lying, or gossip?

Look up James 1:22-25. What does the passage say about the man who hears the Word but fails to act upon the Word?

> *For there is no good tree which produces bad fruit, nor, on the other hand, a bad tree which produces good fruit. For each tree is known by its own fruit. For men do not gather figs from thorns, nor do they pick grapes from a briar bush. The good man out of the good treasure of his heart brings forth what is good; and the evil man out of the evil treasure brings forth what is evil; for his mouth speaks from that which fills his heart.*
> **Luke 6:43-45 (NASB)**

As you re-read the above passage, think about your own behaviors. What do these verses tell you about the origin of your actions?

What do these two passages of Scripture tell you about the importance of the heart?

What does the Bible say about the condition of your heart?

Because heart change is centered on conviction through the Scriptures, we must look to God's view of the heart found in Jeremiah 17:9:

> *The heart is deceitful above all things, and desperately wicked; who can know it?*
> **Jeremiah 17:9 (NKJV)**

The deceitful heart is bent on satisfying "me," having my own way, living life for my pleasures, with "me" at the center of my universe.

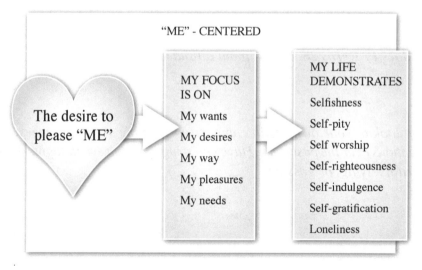

"ME" - CENTERED

The desire to please "ME"

MY FOCUS IS ON
My wants
My desires
My way
My pleasures
My needs

MY LIFE DEMONSTRATES
Selfishness
Self-pity
Self worship
Self-righteousness
Self-indulgence
Self-gratification
Loneliness

Do these things surprise you?

Because the heart has been referred to as the control center of our being, what we think, believe, and desire in our heart is what guides us and can determine our actions. We do not naturally think about our heart being wicked. Many times people are referred to as having a good heart or a big heart. It is possible we have never before heard someone say that our heart is deceitful and wicked and evil. If we are honest with ourselves, we may see that we have some of the sin habits found in Matthew 15:18-20a.

> *But the things that proceed out of the mouth come from the heart, and those defile the man. For out of the heart come evil thoughts, murders, adulteries, fornications, thefts, false witness, slanders. These are the things that defile the man...* **Matthew 15:18-20a (NASB)**

If we are honest with ourselves, we will begin to realize we tend to minimize our sinful heart attitudes; as we read Jesus' words, we see our biggest problem lies within our own hearts.

Question(s) for the reader:

Look up James 4:1 in your Bible. Can you identify the outward visible problem and the inward desires of the heart?

This passage from Romans 1 vividly reveals how our thoughts, beliefs, and desires can guide our actions:

> *... And they began to think up foolish ideas of what God was like. The result was that their minds became dark and confused. Claiming to be wise, they became utter fools instead...So God let them go ahead and do whatever shameful things their hearts desired. As a result, they did vile and degrading things with each other's bodies. Instead of believing what they knew was the truth about God, they deliberately chose to believe lies... God abandoned them to their shameful desires. Even the women turned against the natural way to have sex and instead indulged in sex with each other. And the men, instead of having normal sexual relationships with women, burned with lust for each other. Men did shameful things with other men and, as a result, suffered within themselves the penalty they so richly deserved. When they refused to acknowledge God, he abandoned*

them to their evil minds and let them do things that should never be done. Their lives became full of every kind of wickedness, sin, greed, hate, envy, murder, fighting, deception, malicious behavior, and gossip. They are backstabbers, haters of God, insolent, proud, and boastful. They are forever inventing new ways of sinning and are disobedient to their parents. They refuse to understand, break their promises, and are heartless and unforgiving. They are fully aware of God's death penalty for those who do these things, yet they go right ahead and do them anyway. And, worse yet, they encourage others to do them, too.

Romans 1:21-32 (NLT)

The sins listed in Romans 1:21-32 are results of sinful thoughts, beliefs, and desires. Every action began as a thought; the thought was fueled by a desire or belief; the desire or belief originated in the heart.

Jesus took the opportunity to speak to the attitudes of the heart when He was questioned by the Pharisees and His disciples about pure foods and ceremonial hand washing. He gave this wise reply:

Can't you see that what you eat won't defile you? Food doesn't come in contact with your heart, but only passes through the stomach and then comes out again." (By saying this, he showed that every kind of food is acceptable.) And then he added, "It is the thought-life that defiles you. For from within, out of a person's heart, come evil thoughts, sexual immorality, theft, murder, adultery, greed, wickedness, deceit, eagerness for lustful pleasure, envy, slander, pride, and foolishness. All these vile things come from within; they are what defile you and make you unacceptable to God.

Mark 7:18-23 (NLT)

This is Important!

The vile things that come out from us originated in the heart. Before engaging in sexual immorality, there was a desire for illicit pleasure. Before stealing something, there was a belief that we were entitled to what we wanted and a belief that we would not get caught. Before the adulterous affair, there was the desire to "be happy," to have our needs met, to feel desired by our cohort. Before there was deceit, there was a fear of being caught or exposed. Before we gossiped, we believed we had a right to share that information with someone; we wanted someone else to know.

Where your pleasure is, there is your treasure; where your treasure is, there is your heart; where your heart is, there is your happiness. **Augustine**

Thoughts are an important aspect of the heart

As a man thinks in his heart, so is he.   **Proverbs 23:7 (NLT)**

There is no doubt that our thoughts direct the course of our lives. We base our actions on what we are thinking at the moment and over longer periods of time.

Our thought life is a critical aspect to change in life because what we think or believe about various things will determine how we respond to them. John MacArthur notes:

> The "heart" commonly refers to the mind as the center of thinking and reason, but also includes the emotions, the will and thus the whole inner being. The heart is the depository of all wisdom and the source of whatever affects speech, sight and conduct."

Our thoughts form our opinions, create our belief system, and fan the flame of our desires. What we think determines our emotional mood and causes us to have various feelings. Our thoughts precede our emotions; our emotions and desires are a result of our thought life.

For example, a person who struggles with anxiety may think open-ended thoughts that might begin with a phrase such as, "what if." Most often the "what if" has some root in an aspect of reality. The person's thoughts continue to run along the lines of creating scenarios that are imaginary or merely probable. These thoughts stimulate the body to produce adrenaline, and the person then experiences anxiety.

Desire is born of thought

Just as Eve did in the Garden of Eden when she saw that the fruit was pleasing to the eye, we see something that piques interest in us; we begin the thought process of wondering what it would taste like, how it would feel, and what it would be like to have it. We experience sudden desire, and that desire smolders over time and grows stronger the more we think about the object we want to possess. We then act on our desires, or we set them aside permanently or temporarily.

Thoughts aid in forming beliefs

We take in millions of bits of information and weigh it through the thought process and moral code we have adopted. We conclude that something is true or false, and it then becomes a part of our belief system. Our beliefs stay in place until new information comes along to challenge them.

You see, all of our actions begin as a thought, belief, or desire in our heart.

Before we can change what we habitually do, we must change how we habitually think. Our thoughts and beliefs make up how we "see" sin. If we believe a sin habit is biological or genetic, the most we can do is get long term therapy or take a pill to feel better. We "see" our behavior as not being our fault, and we believe that we are helpless before impulses, thoughts, and drives.

> We do not make a god out of pleasure; we make a god out of whatever we take pleasure in most. Pleasure is not the object of worship; pleasure is the worship.[3]
> **John Piper**

Mind renewal is the critical piece of lasting change

The apostle Paul penned these words:

> *Do not be conformed any longer to the pattern of this world, but be transformed by the renewing of your mind.* **Romans 12:2 (NKJV)**

Before we can change what we do, we have to come to believe or think differently, and that requires a renewing of the mind; in essence, a change of heart.

The Importance of Roots and Fruits

The quality of the fruit of any tree depends on the root system of the tree. When the roots are growing in deep, rich soil full of nutrients, the tree will be strong and healthy. The fruit of that tree will be juicy, sweet, and resistant to bugs and parasites.

The tree rooted in poor quality soil will have little nutrition to carry up through the trunk to the branches and leaves. The tree will be weak and susceptible to disease.

The quality of its fruit will be poor. We could return year after year and pluck the poor fruit from the tree, but that would not change the health of the tree. The tree would remain sickly and vulnerable, bearing bad fruit. The only way to cause a tree to produce good fruit is to attend to the roots. To make application to our life, if we address only the visible problems or our bad feelings (fruit), we will soon return to these problems and feelings in a short time.

Questions for the reader:

What "fruit" do you see in your own life? Is it good fruit or poor fruit? List them.

Have you previously tried to "make" good fruit appear in your life?

What methods did you use?

How successful were your attempts?

How long did it take you to revert back to your old behaviors?

Draw your own tree (using the tree on the next page), including the fruit of your behavior on top and the possible root causes in the ground. Write on the trunk of the tree what you think motivates you to act in this way. This will be harder-hang in there! Remember, all of your actions, including whatever it was that brought you to counseling, began as a thought, belief, or desire in your heart.

Can you see the connection between the desires of your heart (roots) and the behavior (fruit) you are experiencing?

Notes

With this in mind, write a couple of paragraphs explaining your understanding of the relationship between the root and fruit in your life.

What we see as a problem (lying, stealing, anger, pornography) is not the real problem- it is a symptom of the real problem. There is a problem to deal with deeper down in our tree of life. That something has caused our fruit to be bad. We must address the root system because that is where the problem that we see truly begins. We need to deal with our anger, stealing, or depression by attacking the real causes (roots) in a biblical manner. We have to deal with the heart of our problem in order to overcome it. Note that the root system is equal to the heart. For example, if we have the fruit of depression, we have focused our heart on our wants, our perceived needs, our personal rights, our beliefs, and our desires. This results in a self-centered idolatrous heart, which is revealed by our thoughts, words, and actions.

Just as the quality of the fruit of a tree reveals the condition of the soil the tree is rooted in, the condition of our heart will be visible by our words and deeds.

If the heart is not being fed the rich, pure Word of God there will be little spiritual nutrition to help a person to grow and change. A person who is starved of biblical truth will produce poor quality fruit in their Christian life. They will be easily swayed by false teaching, and have difficulty discerning right from wrong. The tree of their life will be weak and the quality of their spiritual fruit will be poor.

Let us use whatever issue(s) we identified in the question above as fruit. Going back to the reasons why fruit is either of good or bad quality, we must conclude that there is a problem to deal with deeper down in our tree of life. Something has caused our fruit to be bad.

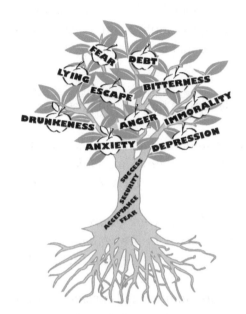

We must return to the root system. In the case of humanity, we can say that the root system is equal to the heart.

What this means is if we have the fruit of anger, depression, anxiety, immorality, drug or alcohol abuse, lying, etc., it is because our roots are embedded in a heart that is not focused on glorifying God. Instead, it is focused on our wants, perceived needs, personal rights, beliefs, and desires. When our heart is not focused on Him but instead is focused on something else, God calls that idolatry.

Identifying Idolatry

You shall have no other gods before me. **Exodus 20:3 (ESV)**
Dear children, keep yourselves from idols. **1 John 5:21 (NIV)**

God considers worship of anything other than Himself idolatry! Look at the following verse:

*When you follow the desires of your sinful nature (your heart), your lives will produce these evil results: sexual immorality, impure thoughts, eagerness for lustful pleasure, **idolatry**, participation in demonic activities, hostility, quarreling, jealousy, outbursts of anger, selfish ambition, divisions, the feeling that everyone is wrong except those in your own little group.* **Galatians 5:19-20 (NLT)**, (author's emphasis)

Each of us struggles with the horrendous sin of idolatry on a daily basis. As Galatians 5 tells us, idolatry is a desire of our sinful nature. It is reflected in our choices, our words, our use of time, and how we spend our money. In our culture we tend to think of idolatry as an eastern religious system such as Buddhism or Hinduism, or as pagan worship of the trees and animals. But the truth is, **idolatry is not only bowing down to statues, it is anything that means more to you than God does**. It is manifested when getting what you want has becomes more important than what God desires for you. Simply put, anything that you are loving, desiring, or serving more than God is an idol of the heart.

> The essence of idolatry is the entertainment of thoughts about God that are unworthy of Him.
> **A.W. Tozer**

We are constantly being tempted to sin in this manner. While many technological advances exist in the world, including new things to idolize and worship, Satan uses the same tricks and methods to bait the trap that he has employed since the Garden of Eden.

Our idolatry takes many forms. Some people idolize money and possessions.

> *People who want to get rich fall into temptation and a trap and into many foolish and harmful desires that plunge men into ruin and destruction.*
> **1 Timothy 6:9 (NIV)**

> *Then he said to them, "Watch out! Be on your guard against all kinds of greed; a man's life does not consist in the abundance of his possessions.*
> **Luke 12:15 (NIV)**

Others idolize people such as celebrities, sports figures, and musicians. Look at the popularity of the program AMERICAN IDOL and the millions of people who watch each week and vote for their "idol."

Criminal rap artists are held in high esteem by the younger generation; the actions of high-priced athletes (who once were lauded for their abilities on the playing field but now are notorious for their antics off the field) are being emulated by high school players.

I (Julie) have known mothers who idolize their children by building a child-centered home. These children grow up believing they are the center of the world, and expect others to cater to their every need and whim; to be idolized by someone else once mom and dad are gone.

Other Gods

What other gods could we have besides the Lord? Plenty. For Israel there were the Canaanite Baals, those jolly natured gods whose worship was a rampage of gluttony, drunkenness, and ritual prostitution. For us there are still the great gods Sex, Shekels, and Stomach (an unholy trinity constituting one god: self), and the other enslaving trio, Pleasure, Possessions, and Position, whose worship is described as *"The lust of the flesh and the lust of the eyes and the pride of life"* (1 John 2:16). Football, the Firm, and Family are also gods for some. Indeed the list of other gods is endless, for anything that anyone allows to run his life becomes his god and the claimants for this prerogative are legion. In the matter of life's basic loyalty, temptation is a many-headed monster.[4]
J.I. Packer

The bottom line is simple—we were born to worship. We have been created to worship God, but our sinful lusts have driven us to worship and idolize the things of the world.

Are you beginning to see how perhaps some of the things we struggle with are from an idolatrous and self-centered heart?

Along the way of our life we came to believe that we needed certain things or people to "make us happy." For some of us it is success or security while for others it is acceptance, and still for others it is motivated by fear. It's a type of fear of not succeeding or being accepted or secure.

These motivations spurred on by the desires of the heart have born exactly the kind of fruit you would expect– awful. If this were not so, people would not seek counseling!

"The evil in our desire typically does not lie in what we want, but that we want it too much."   **John Calvin**

Sometimes the object of desire itself is evil: e.g., to kill someone, to steal, to control the cocaine trade. If the object of desire is good, then the evil lies in the lordship of the desire. Our will replaces God's as that which determines how we live...Natural affections (for any good thing) become inordinate, ruling cravings. We are meant to be ruled by godly passions and desires. Natural desires for good things are meant to exist subordinate to our desire to please the Giver of gifts. The fact that the evil lies in the ruling status of the desire, not the object, is frequently a turning point in counseling.[5]   **C.J.Mahaney**

It is shocking to some counselees that we don't focus on the anger or the drunkenness specifically while counseling. It is not profitable to simply pull the bad fruit off the tree because soon new bad fruit will grow in its place. The consequences you are experiencing are the result of the problem, not **the** problem.

The Doctrine of Radical Amputation

This is not to say that biblical counselors do not take seriously presenting problems such as alcoholism, pornography and other life-dominating sins. In some cases the doctrine of radical amputation must be applied immediately because the consequences of continuing in these habits of the heart can be devastating to the person and others. Jesus said:

> *If your right eye makes you stumble, tear it out and throw it from you; for it is better for you to lose one of the parts of your body, than for your whole body to be thrown into hell. If your right hand makes you stumble,*

53

cut it off and throw it from you; for it is better for you to lose one of the parts of your body, than for your whole body to go into hell.

Matthew 5:29-30 (NASB)

This means that certain presenting problems must be dealt with radically. For example, for the alcoholic, it means a commitment to cease drinking and remove everything from his or her life that tempts them to drink. It can also mean a commitment to detoxification and the cleansing it provides. For the pornography user it means safeguards and accountability for computer usage. It may mean driving a different way home from work lest one be tempted by the adult video stores on the former route.

> "The human heart is a factory of idols...Every one of us is, from his mother's womb, expert in inventing idols."
> **John Calvin**

Radical amputation means doing whatever it takes to stop the destructive behavior, realizing the fruit that was produced has come from the root system of the heart.

We will find the problem where it really lies: in the roots– in our heart

> The first and the great work of a Christian is about his heart. Do not be content with seeming to do good in "outward acts" while your heart is bad, and you are a stranger to the greater internal heart duties.
> **Jonathan Edwards**
>
> You must keep all earthly treasures out of your heart, and let Christ be your treasure, and let Him have your heart. **C.H. Spurgeon**

What guides and motivates our heart is what will change our actions and the resulting fruit.

When our thoughts, beliefs, and desires are set on glorifying God, there will be appropriate actions and God-honoring consequences.

When our heart is set on pleasing "self," our thoughts and actions are not naturally going to be like God's. This presents a dilemma because God commands us in the Bible to be holy.

But now you must be holy in everything you do, just as God-who chose you to be his children-is holy. For he himself has said, "You must be holy because I am holy." **1 Peter 1:15-16 (NLT)**

Practicing holiness brings glory to God. Glorifying God should be the goal of our life. I am often asked by my counselees, "Why am I here?" The simple and straightforward answer to this question could change our life: We are here to glorify God.

Glorifying God happens when the focus of life changes from living for my pleasure and glory to living for His pleasure and glory. It demands that my heart change from a "me-centered" focus to a God-centered focus.

In order to accomplish this goal, changes must take place.

The first change that must take place is in the heart itself. We cannot change our own heart. Because our heart is deceitful and wicked (Jer. 17:9), we cannot possibly know the depths of its depravity, nor can we conjure up enough goodness within ourselves to change in a real and lasting way. We may have tried this before through a New Year's resolution or a "self-help" group of some kind. Our behavior may have changed for a while or to some degree, but studies bear out the fact that merely altering behavior does not bring about lasting and permanent change.

Understanding Our Motive to Change

"He that hath doctrinal knowledge and speculation only, without affection, never is engaged in the business of religion...The holy Scriptures do everywhere place religion very much in the affections...If the Creator has wisely made human nature in this manner, why then misuse our affections? Can we Christians find anything worthier to respond to with all our affections than what is set forth to us in the gospel of Jesus Christ? Can anything be worthier to affect us than this?" **Jonathan Edwards**

We have been divinely enabled to change, to be holy, to live the life God has called us to live! I hope this causes us to shout, "Praise the Lord!"

Often when a person has a problem, their only goal is to feel better. They mistakenly believe that if they feel better or happy that is good enough. We see this often in our counseling ministry. Receiving "good counseling" is equated to what they feel like emotionally during the counseling process. If the emotions are good, then it has been successful. When this is the motive, all too often the problems that brought them to counseling reappear and their sorrow deepens to hopelessness. This is because the goal of the counseling is off-base.

The goal of all counseling is change, but not change in circumstances or change in feelings. The goal of biblical counseling is heart level change that brings about a life that glorifies God.

This means God's priorities become our priorities. What He says in His Word is important to Him and becomes important to us.

These changes take place in the inner man before they are evidenced in behavior.

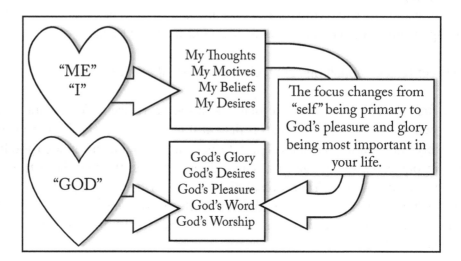

Chapter Five

Inner Man / Inner Life

To be Set Apart for Holy Use

To sanctify means to be set apart for a holy use. God has set us apart for the purpose of sanctification, not impurity, (1 Thess. 4:7) and being such we are called to do good works (Eph. 2:10).

Christians are to sanctify Christ as Lord in their hearts (1 Pet. 3:15). God sanctified Israel as His own special nation (Ezek. 37:28). People can be sanctified (Ex. 19:10, 14); and so can a mountain (Ex. 19:23), and the Sabbath day (Gen. 2:3). Every created thing is sanctified through the Word of God and prayer (1 Tim. 4:4).

Sanctification follows justification. In justification, our sins are completely forgiven in Christ. Sanctification is the process by which the Holy Spirit makes us more like Christ in all that we do, think, and desire. True sanctification is impossible apart from the atoning work of Christ on the cross, because only after our sins are forgiven, can we begin to lead a holy life.   carm.org/dictionary-sanctification

"Sinner" is a present-tense description of everyone, including those who have put their faith in Christ. Of course, those who have called Jesus "Lord" are justified, meaning that they are no longer guilty. Also, they have been given the Spirit, which makes them slaves to Christ rather than to sin. But we all are sinners. Perfection awaits eternity.[1]

The Bible has plenty to say about the workings of the inner man and the resulting behavior. The Bible calls this process sanctification. I would like you to focus on a few key passages to aid you in understanding the process of biblical change.

The first is that we are commanded to change.

> *With the Lord's authority let me say this: Live no longer as the ungodly do, for they are hopelessly confused.*   **Ephesians 4:17 (NLT)**

> *Do not let sin control the way you live; do not give in to its lustful desires. Do not let any part of your body become a tool of wickedness, to be used for sinning. Instead, give yourselves completely to God since you have been given new life. And use your whole body as a tool to do what is right for the glory of God.*   **Romans 6:12-13 (NLT)**

> *Therefore, I urge you, brothers, in view of God's mercy, to offer your bodies as living sacrifices, holy and pleasing to God—this is your spiritual*

act of worship. Do not conform any longer to the pattern of this world, but be transformed by the renewing of your mind. **Romans 12:1-2 (NIV)**

In Romans 12:2, *"the renewing of the mind"* is one aspect of heart change. The word "transformed" in Greek is metamorphoo. We transliterate this word as metamorphosis. (It means to transform (literally or figuratively "metamorphose") to change, transfigure, transform.)[2]

It is most often compared to the caterpillar transforming into the butterfly. At salvation our hearts were transformed from a heart of stone that hated God to a heart of flesh that is capable of loving God (Ezekiel 36:26) and serving and worshipping Him.

Just as the butterfly in no way resembles the caterpillar, we are not to be fashioned like, shaped, or outwardly resemble the world's values, morals, behaviors, and beliefs.

For though your hearts were once full of darkness, now you are full of light from the Lord, and your behavior should show it! For this light within you produces only what is good and right and true.
Ephesians 5:8-9 (NLT)

Daniel Yankelovitch published a book entitled NEW RULES: SEARCHING FOR SELF-FULFILLMENT IN A WORLD TURNED UPSIDE DOWN. He argues on the basis of extensive interviews and nationwide polls that massive shifts have occurred in our culture and that the widespread search for personal self-fulfillment has created a new set of rules that govern the way we think and feel as Americans. He says, "In their extreme form the new rules simply turn the old ones on their head, and in place of the old self-denial ethic we find people who refuse to deny anything to themselves—not out of bottomless appetite, but on the strange moral principle that 'I have a duty to myself.'" (p. xviii). He tells of a young woman in her mid-thirties who complained to her psychotherapist that she was becoming nervous and fretful because life had grown so hectic—too many big weekends, too many discos, too many late hours, too much talk, too much wine, too much pot, too much lovemaking. "Why don't you stop?" asked the therapist mildly. The patient stared blankly for a moment, and then her face lit up, dazzled by an illumination: "You mean I really don't have to do what I want to?" she burst out in amazement. The trademark of the new self-fulfillment seekers is that "they operate on the premise that emotional cravings are sacred objects and that it is a crime against nature to harbor an unfulfilled emotional need" (p. 59). "Ours is the first era when tens of millions of people offer as moral justification for their acts the idea that an inner and presumably more 'real' self does not fit well with their assigned social role."
John Piper

This kind of mind change only comes as the Holy Spirit changes your thinking through consistent study and meditation on the Word of God. This kind of study will enable us to know what God's will is for us.

> *Don't copy the behavior and customs of this world, but let God transform you into a new person by changing the way you think. Then you will know what God wants you to do, and you will know how good and pleasing and perfect his will really is.* **Romans 12:2 (NLT)**

There is no better passage for describing the changes we are to undergo than what we find beginning in Ephesians 4:22:

> *...throw off your old evil nature and your former way of life, which is rotten through and through, full of lust and deception. Instead, there must be a spiritual renewal of your thoughts and attitudes. You must display a new nature because you are a new person, created in God's likeness—righteous, holy, and true.* **Ephesians 4:22-24 (NLT)**

Another version says it this way:

> *...that you put off, concerning your former conduct, the old man which grows corrupt according to the deceitful lusts, and be renewed in the spirit of your mind, and that you put on the new man which was created according to God, in true righteousness and holiness.* **Ephesians 4:22-24 (NKJV)**

What are we to put off?

- Selfish ambition (thinking of yourself before other people)
- Dissentions (trouble causing)
- Factions (causing divisions)
- Envy (wanting what someone else has)
- Drunkenness (alcoholism, drinking to excess)
- Orgies (group sex)
- Unrighteousness (injustice, or iniquity in general)
- Wickedness (a desire of injuring others; malice. Striving to produce injury on others)
- Covetousness (the desire of obtaining what belongs to others)
- Licentiousness (evil in general; rather the act of doing wrong than the desire which was expressed before by the word "wickedness")
- Murder (The taking of human life with premeditated malice by a person of a sane mind.)
- Debate (contention, strife, altercation, connected with anger and heated zeal; This contention and strife would, of course, flow from malice and covetousness, etc.)

Notes

- Deceit (denotes fraud, falsehood)
- Malignity (misinterpreting the words or actions of others, or putting the worst construction on their conduct)
- Whisperers (gossipers, those who secretly, and in a sly manner, by hints and innuendoes, detract from others)
- Wraths (anger or animosities between contending factions, the usual effect of forming parties)
- Strife (between contending factions)
- "Factions" (split up into parties, and those parties were embittered with mutual recriminations and reproaches, as they always are in a church)
- Backbiters (those who slander, or speak ill of those who are absent)
- Haters of God
- Despiteful (this word denotes those who abuse, or treat with unkindness or disdain)
- Proud—Pride is well understood. It is an inordinate self-esteem; an unreasonable conceit of one's superiority in talents, beauty, wealth, accomplishments, etc. (Webster).
- Boasters (those who arrogate to themselves what they do not possess, and glory in it - closely connected with pride)
- Inventors of evil things (seeking to find out new arts or plans to practice evil; new devices to gratify their lusts and passions; new forms of luxury and vice, etc.)
- Disobedient to parents (this expresses the idea that children did not show to parents the honor, respect, and attention which was due)
- Without understanding (inconsiderate or foolish)
- Covenant breakers (false to their contracts)
- Without natural affections (This expression denotes the lack of affectionate regard toward their children. Refers here to the practice of exposing their children, or putting them to death - abortion, infanticide.)
- Unmerciful (destitute of compassion)
- Unrighteous (The unjust - they who did injustice to others and attempted to do it under the sanction of the courts.)
- Effeminate (Applied to morals, as it is here, it denotes those who make self-indulgence the grand object of life; those who are given up to wantonness and sensual pleasures, or who are kept to be prostituted to others.)
- Revilers (coarse, harsh, and bitter words; a man whose characteristic it was to abuse others, to vilify their character, and wound their feelings)
- Thieves (extortionist, persons greedy of gain, and oppressing the poor, the needy, and the fatherless, to obtain money)
- Rioting (reveling, denoting the licentious conduct, the noisy and obstreperous mirth, the scenes of disorder and sensuality, which attend luxurious living)
- Drunkenness (rioting and drunkenness)
- Lewd (immodest behavior - includes illicit indulgences of all kinds, adultery, etc.)
- Strife (envying, contention, disputes, litigation)
- Envying (any intense, vehement, "fervid" passion)

You will find these listed in Galatians 5:19; Romans 1:24-32, 13:13; 1 Corinthians 6:9,10; and Colossians 3:5.

Question(s) for the reader:

As you review this list, do you see any of these sins in your life?

Which ones are new to you?

With which of these sins have you been known to struggle?

What have you done in the past to try and deal with these sins?

Even though you are a Christian, you may struggle with some or many of these sins. You will never be completely free from all sin while on this earth, but by God's grace, as you grow in Christ, you will see a decrease in your sinful habits and an increase in righteous thinking and behavior.

The New King James version of Ephesians 4:22 tells us that the old man "grows corrupt" according to the deceitful lusts. Our flesh (old man, sinful nature) will be with us until the day we leave this earth.

If the flesh is fed, it will continue to flourish and grow stronger and more corrupt. The flesh is not fed by goodness, it is fed by sinful thoughts and desires that lead to sinful actions. Its desires are insatiable.

An excellent illustration of corruption comes from ancient Roman justice. When a man committed murder, one method of punishment was to strap the dead body of the victim to the murderer. The victim would be tied to the murderer at the wrists, chest, legs, and ankles to give maximum skin contact. The murderer would have to carry his victim everywhere he went, there was no escape. As the body of the victim began to decompose, flies would gather and maggots would soon cover the body. Acid from the decomposition would begin to eat into the skin of the murderer opening him up to infection from the flies and other means. The stench from the rotting flesh would nauseate the host, and he would beg for

release from this torture. He would want more than anything to be able to throw off this rotting, stinking corpse and get away. Eventually, the murderer would die of septic shock, blood poisoning, or another infection.

This illustration points us to the fact that the flesh grew more and more corrupt as it stayed in contact with the rotting flesh, to the point that it snuffed the life out of the host.

> *For if you live according to the sinful nature, you will die; but if by the Spirit you put to death the misdeeds of the body, you will live.*
> **Romans 8:13 (NIV)**

Bringing this back to today, the longer we stay in contact with our former way of life and the sin it contained, the more corrupt we will become. We are told to "put off"and "throw off" our former conduct. This implies stripping off, or flinging it far away, as though it were that rotting corpse.

Accompanying putting off the old man is being renewed in the spirit of the mind:

> *Instead, there must be a spiritual renewal of your thoughts and attitudes.* **Ephesians 4:23 (NLT)**

The Word and Spirit supply what is needed to renew the mind (Rom 12:1-2). This is inseparably coupled with changed living and enables us to understand, believe, and obey.

> *...you have stripped off your old evil nature and all its wicked deeds. In its place you have clothed yourselves with a brand-new nature that is continually being renewed as you learn more and more about Christ, who created this new nature within you.* **Colossians 3:9b-10 (NLT)**

When we become a Christian, God gives us a completely new spiritual and moral capacity that a mind apart from Christ could never achieve (1 Corinthians 2:9-16). The mind is the center of thought, understanding, belief, desire, and motivation. This is why it is critical to begin to renew your mind with His Word.

New responses to old temptations is what is required

This commitment to total obedience does not mean a mere negative avoidance of evil practices. It also means positively obeying God's commands. We cannot say that someone is a true Christian just because he is not a thief, liar, blasphemer, drunkard, sexually immoral, arrogant, cruel or fierce. He also has to be positively God-fearing, humble, respectful, gentle, peaceful, forgiving, merciful and loving. Without these positive qualities, he is not obeying the laws of Christ. **Jonathan Edwards**

It is not adequate to just change behavior because what drives the behavior is still the same. Our mind must be retrained to operate biblically so that when we are presented with the same old temptations, we think a new response. Instead of, "If I tell the truth, I am going to be in trouble," the new thought will become, "Telling the truth is the way I will honor God, even if it means I am disciplined. It is more important to be honest than it is to look good or escape being disciplined."

We cannot assume that new thinking alone will lead to walking worthy and new living. We must also deal with what is standing in the way of belief and action. Genuine change is more than stopping wrong behavior; there must be repentance which includes an understanding that the actions are not glorifying to God; there must be a change in the manner of life that we live. Genuine repentance is accompanied by a desire to obey. We cannot separate thinking from obedience- they are inseparable.

> *And remember, it is a message to obey, not just to listen to. If you don't obey, you are only fooling yourself. For if you just listen and don't obey, it is like looking at your face in a mirror but doing nothing to improve your appearance. You see yourself, walk away, and forget what you look like.* **James 1:22-24 (NLT)**

When Jesus Christ is the ruler of our heart (inner man), our thoughts, understanding, beliefs, desires, and motivations flow from what He wants us to do as seen in His Word.

Finally,

> *You must display a new nature* (put on the new self, put on the new man) *because you are a new person, created in God's likeness—righteous, holy, and true.* **Ephesians 4:24 (NLT)** (verse quoted with my additions)

This indicates a change of our entire life-style. Real change begins in our heart and overflows into our lives where Christ is reflected in us.

Specific Examples of Putting Off / Putting On
Ephesians 4 & 5

Put Off	Put On
4:25 Put away lying	Speak truth
4:26 Do not sin in your anger	Don't carry anger overnight, forgive
4:28 Stop stealing	Work for what you need so you can share with others

Put Off	Put On
4:29 stop corrupt speech	Say things that build others up and give grace to the hearer
4:31 put away all bitterness, wrath, anger, loud quarreling, evil speaking	Be kind to others, tenderhearted, forgiving, imitators of God, walk in love, giving thanks
5:3 Fornication, uncleanness, covetousness	5:11 Have no fellowship with the deeds of unrighteousness
5:4 Filthiness, foolish talk, coarse jesting	5:15 Walk carefully, wisely, understanding what God's will is. Manifest the Fruit of the Spirit

Don't be fooled by those who try to excuse these sins, for the terrible anger of God comes upon all those who disobey him. Don't participate in the things these people do. For though your hearts were once full of darkness, now you are full of light from the Lord, and your behavior should show it! For this light within you produces only what is good and right and true. Try to find out what is pleasing to the Lord. Take no part in the worthless deeds of evil and darkness; instead, rebuke and expose them. It is shameful even to talk about the things that ungodly people do in secret.
Ephesians 5:6-12 (NLT)

All these things are possible and required by God. He never tells us what to do without telling us how to do it or equipping us to do it.

Now to him who is able to do immeasurably more than all we ask or imagine, according to his power that is at work within us.
Ephesians 3:20 (NIV)

I am the true vine, and my Father is the gardener. He cuts off every branch that doesn't produce fruit, and he prunes the branches that do bear fruit so they will produce even more. You have already been pruned for greater fruitfulness by the message I have given you. Remain in me, and I will remain in you. For a branch cannot produce fruit if it is severed from the vine, and you cannot be fruitful apart from me. Yes, I am the vine; you are the branches. Those who remain in me, and I in them, will produce much fruit. For apart from me you can do nothing. **John 15:1-5 (NLT)**

For God is working in you, giving you the desire to obey him and the power to do what pleases him. **Philippians 2:13 (NLT)**

Heart change is done by the Spirit of God. The process of sanctification is evidence of our salvation. Were it not for the Holy Spirit living inside us, we would have no desire to change our heart or to glorify God.

This is very important: God is pleased with us because of Christ, and that does not change. His pleasure rests upon us because His wrath has been satisfied for the sake of Christ.

The "pleasing" of God that is done in the sanctification process is glorifying to His name and Person. It is contained in revealing Christ in us to others and introducing them to the character and Person of Christ through us. This brings much glory to God.

Transforming Grace

> Grace is not simply leniency when we have sinned. Grace is the enabling gift of God not to sin. Grace is power, not just pardon. Therefore, the effort we make to obey God is not an effort done in our own strength, but in the strength which God supplies.
> **John Piper**

Grace is given to us because it glorifies God to do so, not because we are deserving, special, or worthy. Have you ever thought about what a marvelous thing it is that God chooses to bring Himself glory by saving us?

God demonstrates grace to us because He is holy and cannot tolerate our sinfulness. I am reading a book that contains a chapter about the holiness of God, and the author says that in the Bible you don't read about the cherubim and seraphim surrounding the throne of God and saying, "wonderful, wonderful, wonderful" or, "faithful, faithful, faithful." They say, "holy, holy, holy" when speaking of God. He is a holy God and we would be foolish to think that sinfulness on any level is acceptable to God.

Our unholiness demanded a stiff redemptive price - the blood of Christ.

Our unholiness is the reason we need grace unto salvation. We are completely and totally unworthy of what we have received.

It is in seeing our unworthiness that we can begin to have a glimpse of just exactly why we are to demonstrate grace to those who have hurt us so deeply.

> We are responsible to obey the will of God, but that we are dependent upon the Holy Spirit for the enabling power to do it.[3]
> **Jerry Bridges**

In those painful relationships when we show grace to those who don't deserve it, it is important to realize it may not make one bit of difference in how we are treated by them, and it may not change any manner of response by the offender.

65

What we will experience is freedom from bitterness. In spite of the rotten way we may continue to be treated, we will see God working in our lives as a result of responding in a Christ-like manner.

When helping others to understand this, make it a goal to help them to get their focus off "self" and onto what God is doing in their heart and life as they step out in faith and obedience to the call of Christ.

Remind them the goal is not to end the suffering, but to glorify God as they are suffering.

God's Grace is Sufficient

> Before we can learn the sufficiency of God's grace, we must learn the insufficiency of ourselves. The more we see our sinfulness, the more we appreciate grace in its basic meaning of God's undeserved favor. In a similar manner, the more we see our frailty, weakness, and dependence, the more we appreciate God's grace in its dimension of His divine assistance. Just as grace shines more brilliantly against the dark background of our sin, so it also shines more brilliantly against the background of our human weakness.[4]
> **Jerry Bridges**

> *And God is able to make all grace abound toward you, that you, always having all sufficiency in all things, may have an abundance for every good work.* **2 Corinthians 9:8 (NKJV)**

> *And He said to me, "My grace is sufficient for you, for My strength is made perfect in weakness."* **2 Corinthians 12:9 (NKJV)**

Grace is sufficient. So many times I hear people say they don't think they can do it - they can't bear up under the strain or under the persecution. They tell me how weak they are. I tell them to rejoice in that weakness! Because then they can really see that it is not them doing it - it is Christ! The grace of God is enough to carry them through!

Grace is sufficient, and it is enough. If it were not enough, God would have made a better provision.

I also have to remind myself that God's grace will be present in abundance when I need it and not before. I cannot store up grace for a rainy day like I can my pennies; it will be sufficient and not lacking anything in that moment.

Realization of Grace

> *For sin shall not have dominion over you, for you are not under law but under grace.* **Romans 6:14 (NKJV)**

I really love this passage of Scripture. When I first realized this, I think I about flew out of my seat!

Romans 6:1 says, *"Are we to continue to live as though we are still slaves to sin? How can we who have been freed from sin still live as though we are still owned by it."*

Realizing that grace is in my life changes my perspective on things, people and circumstances.

When I view all of life through the lens of God's grace demonstrated toward me, I have no other alternative than to change how I live.

Some may disagree with my statement because of the issue of free will. My position is that a true believer will change. They just will! No will of man can overcome the power of the living God; some may change slower than others, but all of us will be changed.

In efficacious grace we are not merely passive, nor yet does God do some and we do the rest. But God does all, and we do all. God produces all, we act all. For that is what produces, viz. our own acts. God is the only proper author and fountain; we only are the proper actors. We are in different respects, wholly passive and wholly active.   **Jonathan Edwards**

Yet the duties God requires of us are not in proportion to the strength we possess in ourselves. Rather, they are proportional to the resources available to us in Christ. We do not have the ability in ourselves to accomplish the least of God's tasks. This is a law of grace. When we recognize it is impossible to perform a duty in our own strength, we will discover the secret of its accomplishment. But alas, this is a secret we often fail to discover.
John Owen, SIN AND TEMPTATION

When the sinner, through the power of the Holy Spirit, begins to understand the enormity of what grace has done for them, their desire becomes one of change to bring Him glory.

If the desire to change is not present, then we will question the validity of the salvation testimony.

When we realize that we are now free from all of the " I have to" in committing sin, our perspective on that sin changes immediately.

Questions for the reader:
If I no longer "have to" sin, then why do I?

Notes

If sin no longer owns me because of grace, then why do I still sin?

I have no choice but to conclude that I sin because I like its temporary results; I like the rush, the immediate gratification, and the clandestine feeling that I am getting away with something.

I deceive myself by thinking sin brings me pleasure when in reality it does not. It is not true pleasure; it is not pleasure without guilty feelings. This is because always after the immediate gratification comes the immediate understanding that I have taken this wonderful grace and abused it, trampling it carelessly.

This is the realization of grace - the understanding that God has given us this wonderful gift that I surely do not deserve and has not given me all the misery I do deserve. He has brought me into His kingdom as His child and given me the riches of this kingdom, lifting me out of slavery and misery, giving me His inheritance. The realization that these things are true about me and cannot be revoked or taken away by anyone causes me to fall down and worship Him. It also causes me to live out this worship in life and demonstrate it to others.

Chapter Six

Understanding Change is a Battle

> The manual of operation for the Christian war-time mentality is the Bible. It was inspired and authorized by the Commander, and contains all the truth needed to win people over from the enemy camp, deprogram their old thought patterns, train them in strategies of righteousness and equip them with armor and weapons to defeat Satan and liberate his captives.[1]
> **John Piper**

Frequently, counselees ask me for practical ways to change. Previously it has been stated in this book that all true change begins in the heart. Religiously following a list of "how to-s" will not produce true change; it may not necessarily change the heart. It may help a person to become a better Pharisee, but over time their true heart condition will be revealed. The suggestions that follow are a display of the heart that desires to change.

You will notice there are no *Questions for the Reader* in this chapter. The suggestions that follow are a display of the heart that desires to change. We recommend completing as many of these practical application items as possible. When applied to the heart, you will benefit greatly!

When a person ceases their love affair with their sin and has begun to view their sin with distain or even hatred, these things are the most effective.

Following are biblical suggestions you can share with those who are looking for practical application:

1. Ask yourself if your thoughts, words, actions, or desires are glorifying to God before you do them.

I suggest making index cards that say, "Does this _____ glorify God?" and place them on your mirrors, books, dashboard, workspace, television or computer monitor. Literally, put them any place that you know you are prone to sin as a reminder of what you are trying to do. This has proven to be a very helpful tool in the early days of change to keep the mind focused in the right direction and to catch one's self in automatic behavior.

> Ken Sande in THE PEACEMAKER maintains that conflict begins in the heart as does all idolatry. In the book he lists a number of x-ray questions that we can ask ourselves to help us determine when even a good desire can turn into the idol of sinful demand.

The questions are:

> •What am I preoccupied with? What is the first thing on my mind in the morning and the last thing on my mind at night?
> •How would I answer the question: "If only _____, then I would be happy, fulfilled, and secure?"
> •What do I want to preserve or to avoid at all costs?
> •Where do I put my trust?
> •What do I fear?
> •When a certain desire is not met, do I feel frustration, anxiety, resentment, bitterness, anger, or depression?
> •Is there something I desire so much that I am willing to disappoint or hurt others in order to have it?[2]
>
> **Ken Sande**

2. Memorize Scripture that specifically relates to the sin that you struggle with.

Writing out these applicable verses on cards and putting them together in a flip chart can be helpful. They are easily portable, fit in a pocket, purse, or book bag and can be used anywhere. Repetition is the most effective way to memorize, so frequent readings of these cards will be very helpful.

> *How can a young man keep his way pure? By guarding it according to your word. With my whole heart I seek you; let me not wander from your commandments! I have stored up your word in my heart, that I might not sin against you.* **Psalm 119:9-11 (ESV)**

3. Think about your thoughts

> The mind is a garden that could be cultivated to produce the harvest that we desire.
> The mind is a workshop where the important decisions of life and eternity are made.
> The mind is an armory where we forge the weapons for our victory or our destruction.
> The mind is a battlefield where all the decisive battles of life are won or lost. **Source unknown**

On the surface this may appear odd, but thinking about what you are thinking about is actually a critical step in mind renewal. Begin by asking God to search you and know your heart.

> *Search me, O God, and know my heart; test me and know my thoughts. Point out anything in me that offends you, and lead me along the path of everlasting life.* **Psalm 139:23-24 (NLT)**

Be comforted in the truth that God is all-knowing. There is nothing that God does not know about you; you cannot shock Him. He knows what is in your heart before you do; He is acquainted with all your ways. God's desire is that you are aware of the thoughts that must be changed. King David said this:

> *O LORD, you have examined my heart and know everything about me. You know when I sit down or stand up. You know my every thought when far away. You chart the path ahead of me and tell me where to stop and rest. Every moment you know where I am. You know what I am going to say even before I say it, LORD.* **Psalm 139:1-4 (NLT)**

This request is a sign of humility and submission to Who He is. To ask God to see if there is any wickedness in you, indicates your desire to change.

4. Confess your sin to God.

> *If we say we have no sin, we are only fooling ourselves and refusing to accept the truth. But if we confess our sins to him, he is faithful and just to forgive us and to cleanse us from every wrong.* **1 John 1:8-9 (NLT)**

Admitting you sin is a sign of the Holy Spirit working within you.

Confession is agreeing with God that what you have done is wrong and is offensive to Him. When you know you have done wrong, you are responsible to change your behavior through the renewing of your mind.

5. Try keeping a thought journal.

Initially, this may be a struggle for you. Typically, I receive resistance to keeping the journal, but I tell you it is one of the <u>most effective tools</u> for change. The objections for this activity tend to be along the lines of struggling with putting thoughts on paper, and this is exactly why it is so effective. Those who struggle with automatic behavior are not actively thinking, they are reacting to long-standing habits and behaviors.

These reactions are comfortable for them, and I am often told that the counselee feels awkward putting this on paper. All the more reason to do this project!

I suggest writing down what you are thinking, believing, and desiring in your heart throughout the day, especially during times when you have sinned or want to sin. Then, review the journal and see if you can support your thoughts, beliefs, or desires biblically. The goal in this assignment is to help you see your thoughts in an objective manner. See if you can find Scripture that contextually supports your thoughts or reveals that you were wrong and sinned. Confess your sin to God, thank Him for His forgiveness, and seek to memorize the verses that speak to your specific sinful struggles to help you overcome them.

6. Take every thought captive

> (Spiritual strongholds) begin with a thought. One thought becomes a consideration. A consideration develops into an attitude, which leads then to action. Action repeated becomes a habit, and a habit establishes a "power base for the enemy," that is, a stronghold. [3]   **Elisabeth Elliot**

> Always remember that what you think in your heart is what drives your behavior.

> *We demolish arguments and every pretension that sets itself up against the knowledge of God, and we take captive every thought to make it obedient to Christ.*
> **2 Corinthians 10:5 (NIV)**

When you are beginning the process of mind renewal, there are many old thought patterns to be battled with. You cannot conquer your thought-life with traditional weapons; your battle takes place in the unseen world of your mind and heart.

While turning off the TV or leaving corrupting company is a tangible way to do battle, the bulk of this war is internal. It is a war.

You must assault your old and sinful thought patterns with the truth of God's Word. You must capture these thoughts and subject them to biblical scrutiny. Do they pass the test of heart change? Do they past the test of glorifying God?

The above verse says you must *"demolish arguments (thoughts, ideas, speculations, reasonings, philosophies, and false religions) and every pretension that sets itself up (exalts itself) against the knowledge of God."*(amplification added)

This is a battle that takes place in the mind– and you can expect a battle! You may have been living with sinful thought patterns for many years. Is it reasonable to expect your thoughts to rapidly change?

Indeed, some change may come easily; but, some of your behaviors, thoughts, and desires will not be so easily changed.

> *The old sinful nature loves to do evil, which is just opposite from what the Holy Spirit wants. And the Spirit gives us desires that are opposite from what the sinful nature desires. These two forces are constantly fighting each other, and your choices are never free from this conflict.*
> **Galatians 5:17 (NLT)**

These two natures are at war with each other; they desire opposite things. The flesh will lead you toward sinful behavior; the Spirit will remind you of what is right and what God desires - obedience that glorifies Him.

This will be an ongoing war until you reach glory.

> Resolved, never to give over, nor in the least to slacken, my fight with my corruptions, however unsuccessful I may be.
>
> **Jonathan Edwards**
> **Resolution Number 56.**

7. Habits can be broken.

Since these are sinful habits, they can be changed. Thank God that these are not illnesses, defects, or disorders. What you struggle with is sin. Sin is serious, but not insurmountable! Your sin is serious enough that Jesus Christ died for it and gave you victory over it. You no longer have to live your life in slavery to your current sinful thoughts, beliefs, and desires.

> *But remember that the temptations that come into your life are no different from what others experience. And God is faithful. He will keep the temptation from becoming so strong that you can't stand up against it. When you are tempted, He will show you a way out so that you will not give in to it.* **1 Corinthians 10:13 (NLT)**

There will be times when you fail to take the way of escape God has provided and you fall back into the sinful habit you were trying to put off; just remember that change takes time and this is a process. You didn't develop this habit over night, and you may not conquer it over night either. With consistent application of what you have learned, there will be steady and measurable progress.

8. Take Heart.

> Confidence in the sovereignty of God in all that affects us is crucial to our trusting Him. If there is a single event in all of the universe that can occur outside of God's sovereign control, then we cannot trust Him. His love may be infinite, but if His power is limited and His purpose can be thwarted, we cannot trust Him.[4] **Jerry Bridges**

Wherever you find yourself in this change process, please be assured that you are exactly where God wants you to be. God is never surprised at your sin or your struggles with it. He never wastes anything, even our failures.

> *And we know that God causes everything to work together for the good of those who love God and are called according to his purpose for them. For God knew his people in advance, and he chose them to become like his Son, so that his Son would be the firstborn, with many brothers and*

Notes

sisters. And having chosen them, he called them to come to him. And he gave them right standing with himself, and he promised them his glory.

Romans 8:28-30 (NLT)

All of these things are a part of what God is doing in and through you.

Be encouraged! Jesus Christ has provided the victory for you! The victory is yours for the taking! Because of who you are in Christ, you have the ability to change, and even greater than that, you have the God of the universe assisting you, caring for you, and loving you. This should bring you tremendous hope!

By the power of God, there is nothing that cannot be changed!

Now to him who is able to do immeasurably (exceedingly, abundantly, infinitely) more than all we ask or imagine, according to his power that is at work within us, may he be given glory in the church and in Christ Jesus forever and ever through endless ages. Amen.

Ephesians 3:20-21 (NIV) (amplifications added)

Section III

Understanding the Specific Habits of the Heart That Need to Change

Chapter Seven

Understanding the Heart of Idolatry

The heart of idolatry is truly central to most of the issues we face in life and in helping people who want to change. Just like other sins that we struggle with, idolatry is rooted in the immaterial part of man we refer to as the heart. The heart contains your thoughts, beliefs, desires, mind, will, and emotions. This is why the heart can be referred to as the processing center of your being. The heart of mankind is deceitful and wicked according to Jeremiah 17:9, and the sinful nature that we battle feeds the wicked desires of the heart.

> *When you follow the desires of your sinful nature, your lives will produce these evil results: sexual immorality, impure thoughts, eagerness for lustful pleasure, idolatry, participation in demonic activities, hostility, quarreling, jealousy, outbursts of anger, selfish ambition, divisions, the feeling that everyone is wrong except those in your own little group.* **Galatians 5:19-20 (NLT)**

Let us, then, have it fixed down in our minds that the sinfulness of man does not begin from without, but from within. It is not the result of bad training in early years. It is not picked up from bad companions and bad examples, as some weak Christians are too fond of saying. No! It is a family disease, which we all inherit from our first parents, Adam and Eve, and with which we are born.

J.C. Ryle

Obviously, idolatry is nothing new. We can look back to Genesis 3 to see the origins of this sinful problem.

> *Now the serpent was the shrewdest of all the creatures the LORD God had made. "Really?" he asked the woman. "Did God really say you must not eat any of the fruit in the garden?"*

Satan planted doubt in the mind of the woman about what God had said.

> *"Of course we may eat it," the woman told him. "It's only the fruit from the tree at the center of the garden that we are not allowed to eat. God says we must not eat it or even touch it, or we will die."*

> *"You won't die!" the serpent hissed. "God knows that your eyes will be opened when you eat it. You will become just like God, knowing everything, both good and evil."*

The big lie occurs here, and the great temptation—"You will be like God." Man has wanted to be his own god since that time. Being your own god means freedom from accountability.

> *The woman was convinced. The fruit looked so fresh and delicious, and it would make her so wise! So she ate some of the fruit. She also gave some to her husband, who was with her. Then he ate it, too. At that moment, their eyes were opened, and they suddenly felt shame at their nakedness. So they strung fig leaves together around their hips to cover themselves.* **Genesis 3:1-7 (NLT)**

Thus they succumbed to the lust of the eyes, the lust of the flesh, and the pride of life. Sin and guilt entered the world, and to this day Satan uses the same tactics against us. We see this reiterated in John's first epistle to the churches.

> *For the world offers only the lust for physical pleasure, the lust for everything we see, and pride in our possessions. These are not from the Father. They are from this evil world.* **1 John 2:16 (NLT)**

Our daily newspapers are full of stories of those who have lied, cheated, stolen, prostituted themselves, sold drugs, and even murdered for physical pleasures. However, a far greater number of people unnecessarily abandon their homes and children for the pursuit of money on a daily basis.

> The God of this world is riches, pleasure and pride.
> **Martin Luther**

These actions violate numerous portions of Scripture and indicate that temporal things and the acquisition of them are worthy of throwing spiritual growth aside. Those that struggle in this area have decided that their identities lie in their wealth and possessions.

Questions for the reader:
What are some things you recognize as idols in your life?

Prior to this, had you recognized your idolatrous worship of these people and/or things?

Thank God we have a High Priest who sympathizes with us in our weakness! After fasting for forty days in the wilderness, Jesus Christ was presented by Satan with a choice to sin in idolatry.

> *Next the Devil took him to the peak of a very high mountain and showed him the nations of the world and all their glory. "I will give it all to you," he said, "if you will only kneel down and worship me." "Get out of here, Satan," Jesus told him. "For the Scriptures say, 'You must worship the Lord your God; serve only him.'"* **Matthew 4:8-10 (NLT)**

Christ is the desire of nations, the joy of angels, the delight of the Father. What solace then must that soul be filled with, that has the possession of Him to all eternity! **John Bunyan**

Serving only Him means that we deny our urge to idolize things and people. God made things available for us to enjoy and placed people in our life to love because this glorifies Him. We are not to worship or build our life around them, and those people and things certainly are not to replace our love for the Lord. As we may have already discovered, when our goals, dreams, and desires are in conflict with God's, we will experience sorrow. God's desire for us is to glorify Him, to live a life that honors and serves Him.

Whatever we worship or place a high value on is what we serve and obey. God hates idolatry.

Questions for the reader:

Have you experienced sorrow as a result of the deception of idolatry? Take a moment and write out how it has affected your life.

There are hundreds of verses in the Bible that tell us of the hatred God has for those who worship anything or anyone other than Him.

Isaiah 44 gives us a picture of how our foolishness can easily lead us into idolatry. In this passage we find the woodsman who plants a tree and tends to it. God provides the rich soil and rain to nourish the tree, and the sun provides the light it needs to grow strong and tall. The woodsman cuts down the tree and uses part of it for firewood to roast the meat God has provided...

Then he takes what's left and makes his god: a carved idol! He falls down in front of it, worshiping and praying to it. "Rescue me!" he says. "You are my god!" Such stupidity and ignorance! Their eyes are closed, and they cannot see. Their minds are shut, and they cannot think. The person who made the idol never stops to reflect, "Why, it's just a block of wood! I burned half of it for heat and used it to bake my bread and roast my meat. How can the rest of it be a god? Should I bow down to worship a chunk of wood?" The poor, deluded fool feeds on ashes. He is trusting something that can give him no help at all. Yet he cannot bring himself to ask, "Is this thing, this idol that I'm holding in my hand, a lie?"

Isaiah 44:17-20 (NLT)

Questions for the reader:

Are the people and things you hold onto intended to rescue you, meet your needs, and make you feel better?

Are the things you worship really just ashes?

Are they going to save you from your felt needs?

We must begin to ask ourselves whether what we are holding onto, this worship of self, is a lie.

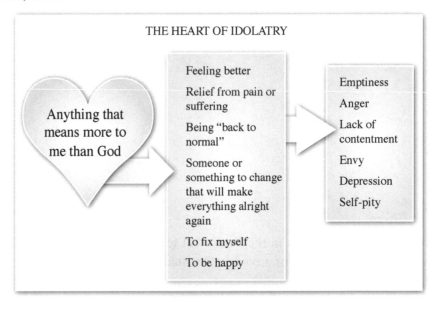

THE HEART OF IDOLATRY

Anything that means more to me than God

- Feeling better
- Relief from pain or suffering
- Being "back to normal"
- Someone or something to change that will make everything alright again
- To fix myself
- To be happy

- Emptiness
- Anger
- Lack of contentment
- Envy
- Depression
- Self-pity

These desires are not wrong, but they can become idols if they come to mean more to us than living our life to glorify, worship and serve God, as well as minister to others.

A good indication that idolatry is present in our lives is when we are willing to sin to get what we want.

Question for the reader:
Are you willing to sin to get relief from pain, to be happy, or to attain any of the other feelings mentioned above?

Can you say why this is so important to you?

If having our felt needs met has become so important to us that we are willing to violate God's Word to have them, then we have crossed the line from desire to worship.

> I find myself frequently depressed- perhaps more so than any other person here. And I find no better cure for that depression than to trust in the Lord with all my heart, and seek to realize afresh the power of the peace-speaking blood of Jesus, and His infinite love in dying upon the cross to put away all my transgressions.
>
> **C.H. Spurgeon**

Let us look at a common example from everyday life:

Many people today complain about feelings of depression, and this issue seems to dominate the lives of a large segment of our counseling cases. One of our goals is to help them understand that their struggle with depression is the result of idolizing self.

People who are depressed typically focus on the desire to feel better. Feeling better is the total focus of every day, and it becomes the goal, the recurring thought, the overwhelming driving force of every day. This desire is so self-focused that it leaves no room for them to see what God may be accomplishing in them and through them during this time. The focus on self leaves no room for worship of God. Unfortunately, this self-focused desire is fed by ads in magazines, on billboards, and on television that leads them to believe it is not okay to feel sad, unhappy, or "bad."

When the depression does not lift despite their pleadings with God, the focus on self becomes even more intense. They often begin to question the goodness of God, the righteousness of God, and the sovereignty of God.

They fail to realize that God often uses internal pain to alert us to something that He wants to change in our hearts. We must not run from the pain. James says:

> *Whenever trouble comes your way, let it be an opportunity for joy. For when your faith is tested, your endurance has a chance to grow. So let it grow, for when your endurance is fully developed, you will be strong in character and ready for anything.* **James 1:2-4 (NLT)**

It may be difficult for us, including those who are depressed, to see ourselves as people who have idols of the heart. We simply don't think that way unless the Word of God penetrates our self-deception and the Holy Spirit reveals it to us. I have presented a good case for why a depressed person may fit in the category of an idolater; I would urge you to go to God right now and ask Him to reveal to you if indeed you are one who struggles with this sin.

A second common issue is sexual immorality. Those involved in pornography, fornication (sex outside of marriage), or masturbation are participating in idolatry of the heart.

No sin that a person commits has more built-in pitfalls, problems and destructiveness than sexual sin. It has broken more marriages, shattered more homes, caused more heartache and disease, and destroyed more lives than alcohol and drugs combined. It causes lying, stealing, cheating and killing, as well as bitterness, hatred, slander, gossip and unforgiveness.[1]

John MacArthur

Their felt needs demand to be satisfied at any cost! When a person participates in any of these immoral behaviors, he or she is committing idolatry. There is no thought of how their actions will affect their spouse or the heartache that will ensue; their only thoughts are of their ability to get what they want at any cost.

> *Flee immorality. Every other sin that a man commits is outside the body, but the immoral man sins against his own body.* **1 Corinthians 6:18 (NASB)**

This entire passage speaks to the importance of purity in the body. In 1 Corinthians 5:9-11, Paul says that sexual immorality is idolatry!

Putting Off the Heart of Idolatry

We are instructed to turn from godless living and sinful pleasures. We should live in this evil world with self-control, right conduct, and devotion to God, while we look forward to that wonderful event when the glory of our great God and Savior, Jesus Christ, will be revealed.
Titus 2:12-13 (NLT)

Therefore, my beloved, flee from idolatry. **1 Corinthians 10:14 (NKJV)**

Dear children, keep away from anything that might take God's place in your hearts. **1 John 5:21 (NLT)**

These must be the desires of anyone who wants true change. At this point I would suggest you make confession to God for your idolatry. Follow up with a prayer of repentance and, finally, develop actions that demonstrate the fruit of repentance. I suggest trying the following actions:

•Begin to admit the sin of idolatry exists in the heart. Admission is the first step, but removing the idols of the heart and life is an ongoing process.

There is a space below to write out the things known to be idols of the heart and life. Place them in the first column. In the second column, write out the Scripture verses that apply specifically to the process of renewing the mind concerning this idol. In the third column write out a plan of action to overcome the habit of indulging self in this way. The plan must be concrete and specific such as: "When I am tempted to _____ I will get up and take my Scripture memory cards with me and go outside and walk around the block two times reciting the verses as I walk."

IDOLS	VERSES THAT APPLY	PLAN OF ACTION

IDOLS	VERSES THAT APPLY	PLAN OF ACTION

Please remember, if you have struggled with idolatry for a long time, there are deeply engrained habits. You will be admitting and confessing this sin frequently, but it is important that you do not become discouraged! Recognize that God is working to clean out the deception in your heart.

It is helpful to identify exactly what a person wants that they are not getting and write it down on paper. Some examples would be feeling better or having a better day.

"I want..." (enter your wants)

"I am not getting..."

Often idolatry and anger/bitterness are intermingled. Identifying it on paper will help you to look at it objectively and to view it in the light of God's Word.

Identify if the desire is biblical. You must be able to support it with Scripture (in context). This is important because emotions can lead you to justify your desire for certain things. Yet your feelings prove unreliable as a method of living life to glorify God.

MY DESIRE	BIBLICAL SUPPORT

We often wrongly believe we "deserve" things for unbiblical reasons. Our wrong beliefs can lead us to wrong emotions.

Place those desires and wants on the altar of sacrifice to God.

This is the action step of change. We can do all of the above, but if we do not take this most important step of acting on our new beliefs or understandings, then the rest is useless. Please do not fall into the trap of thinking that just knowing about it is enough; we must act on what is right!

> *And so, dear brothers and sisters, I plead with you to give your bodies to God. Let them be a living and holy sacrifice—the kind he will accept. When you think of what he has done for you, is this too much to ask? Don't copy the behavior and customs of this world, but let God transform you into a new person by changing the way you think. Then you will know what God wants you to do, and you will know how good and pleasing and perfect his will really is.* **Romans 12:1-2 (NLT)**

God wants to change the way we think, which will change the way we live. Daily we need to reject the thoughts of what we want and desire. Begin to obey God by fulfilling the "one another" commands of Scripture. Take the focus off self, begin to live for Christ, and serve family, church, or friends.

Cultivating a Heart of Worship

> Do not look to your hope, but to Christ, the source of your hope.
> **C.H. Spurgeon**

The idolater has had little difficulty with worship - it is just that the object of worship is wrongly directed. We have provided Scriptural admonition and some practical application for action, but how can one be taught to fall in love with God?

The short answer is we can't! Numerous passages in the Old Testament recount God commanding Israel to love Him (Deut. 6:5; 11:1, 13, 22; 13:3; 19:9; 30:6, 16; Josh. 22:5; 23:11) and to demonstrate their love by being faithful to Him and worshiping Him only. They were a dismal failure at this! We are incapable of worshiping God or loving Him without the enablement of the Holy Spirit.

Allow me to draw you a word picture what this might look like. We are to display the evidence of the love of Christ in our actions. This love should well up within us like a geyser and overflow onto the lives of others! Because of all that Christ has done for us, and all that we are in Christ, we are to continually reflect glory to God through worship as we obey the Word, serve others, demonstrate forbearance, overlook hurtful offenses and so on. This is worship as we passionately live life for His glory!

Often those people who benefit from the reflection of our love for Jesus Christ are people who we have conflict with: our spouses with whom we have discord, children who are ungrateful, or co-workers and employers who take advantage of us. Our view of their response to our graciousness changes radically when our motive for doing these things changes. You see, if I am serving others for the glory of God, then does it matter if I am appreciated? If I am obeying and submitting to a harsh authority because of Christ, and because it pleases Him, then is it going to be bearable?

I maintain that when my goal for all I do in life is to glorify God then nothing else matters. God receives my spiritual acts of worship (Romans 12:1), and I experience joy because man's response just doesn't matter any more! It has ceased to be about **me** and **my** feelings and **my** wants and **my** perceived needs, and it is now all about **Him**. It is how I can bring **Him** glory in living my daily life.

Questions for the reader:
Are you "in love" with God?

If not, what is keeping you from loving Him? Take some time and meditate on this question!

If you can say, "Yes, I am in love with God!" what is the basis for your answer?

Too often what we call "love" is fear of punishment, condemnation, and the wrath of God. This kind of obedience is not born out of a heart that desires to worship, it comes from a heart that is terrified. Conscious or not, this kind of obedience is self-oriented and is possibly another outflow of idolatry!

This is not the love that God desires for His people, for He has said,

> *There is no fear in love; but perfect love casts out fear, because fear involves punishment, and the one who fears is not perfected in love.*
> **1 John 4:18 (NASB)**

> We have been enabled to worship Him without fear.
> **(Hebrews 4:16)**

God has made it possible for us to love Him genuinely and truly through Jesus Christ. We have the very same access to the throne of God, the very same Spirit, and the very same fellowship with God the Father, as His Son Jesus Christ does!

As one who used to live this way, I can tell you that you have no idea what freedom there is in living for Him! I am freed from the shackles of performance-oriented Christianity. I understand that God's love for me is not based on anything that I have done; it is based on His love for Jesus who died for me and set me free.

Questions for the reader:

Are these things revelations to you? Have you been a person bound by fear of God?

As you let these words sink into your heart, how do they change your thoughts?

As we live for Him, we no longer have a fear of man. When we behave in ways that are God-focused, all those around us reap the harvest of our love for God and our obedience to His Word.

> *Worship begins with a new desire - a desire to be transformed by the renewing of your mind* **Romans 12:2 (NLT)**

We must ask God to give us more and more desire for Him than for any other worldly thing; to change us from people following the desire to worship and indulge self to people who desire God.

Strong affections for God, rooted in and shaped by the truth of Scripture – this is the bone and marrow of biblical worship.[2]

John Piper

A heart of worship understands fleshly desires are strong but is willing to fight against the desires. A heart of worship does battle with "self."

It says: I want what I want, but I want to glorify God more!

I know this is a struggle, but I have the victory in Christ!

My flesh cries out to be indulged, but I want to resist!

We must ask God to increase our faith and believe we can change, and that this is a better way of life because it glorifies God.

Be determined to look at every situation and challenge through His eyes.

Preach the truth to yourself about feelings, and start dealing with them biblically!

Questions for the reader:
Will you ask God to increase your faith?

Will you look at every situation and challenge through His eyes instead of only looking at the circumstances?

Will you begin to preach the truth to yourself about those feelings and begin to deal with them biblically?

Of course, this new way of life is going to be difficult at times. We are changing the mind and all that goes along with the heart. This involves new thoughts, beliefs, desires, emotions, will, wants, perceived needs, and so on.

Be especially aware of reverting back to old patterns when upset, tired, sick, or stressed. Be aware that when the pot is under stress, that is when the cracks appear.

Be encouraged! God promises to finish what He began when He saved each of us, and nothing about all these months or years is wasted - God uses every moment!

Chapter Eight

Understanding the Heart of Anger

> Love to God is opposite to a disposition in men to be angry at others' faults chiefly as they themselves are offended and injured by them: It rather disposes them to look at them chiefly as committed against God.[1]
> **Jonathan Edwards**
> The Spirit of Love the Opposite of An Angry
> or Wrathful Spirit, 1 Corinthians 13:5.

A wise man fears the LORD and shuns evil, but a fool is hotheaded and reckless. A quick-tempered man does foolish things, and a crafty man is hated. **Proverbs 14:16-17 (NIV)**

An angry man stirs up dissension, and a hot-tempered one commits many sins. **Proverbs 29:22 (NIV)**

Because the heart is self-centered and idolatrous, we can conclude that it is at the root of sinful anger. **Ecclesiastes 7:9 (NLT)**

We live in a society that screams constantly about "rights." when our perceived rights are violated, we become angry.

Women champion their "right to choose;" homosexuals fight for the rights of marriage; children claim a right to privacy; husbands claim a right to sexual relations. How many of these are biblical rights?

Let's examine some of these common perceived rights:[1]
- Right to have and express personal opinions
- Right to respect
- Right to be understood
- Right to have good health
- Right to be appreciated
- Right to be treated fairly
- Right to belong, to be loved, to be accepted
- Right to make your own decisions
- Right to determine your own future
- Right to be considered worthwhile and important
- Right to be protected and cared for
- Right to have fun
- Right to security and safety
- Right to have others obey you
- Right to have your own way
- Right to be free from difficulties and problems

Questions for the reader:
How many of these have you considered or felt were your "right?"

List them below and then support them with Scripture.

Regarding those that you are unable to scripturally support, what is it that causes you to become angry?

Often people want to control God and make Him do things their way. What they believe is that God's will violates their perceived rights. When He makes decisions they don't like, they become angry. The anger is sometimes internalized, and the result is self-pity because God is not doing things their way. Angry people do not understand the sovereignty of God, or if they do understand it, they refuse to accept it.

Such thoughts reveal a prideful, idolatrous heart. Believing we can override the sovereignty of God is untrue and leads to anger, bitterness, and eventually feelings of depression. In fact, depression is anger turned inward. When a person becomes angry and does not repent of it or address it biblically, depression is the result.

> Uncontrolled temper is soon dissipated on others. Resentment, bitterness, and self-pity build up inside our hearts and eat away at our spiritual lives like a slowly spreading cancer.[2]
>
> **Jerry Bridges**

The typical angry response comes from something a person wants and didn't get, or they are angry about something they got and didn't want; but in both cases, they have never dealt with the anger biblically. These kinds of thoughts are what fuel the sinfully angry person's responses. This is why anger ruins relationships, and is at the root of marriage problems, parent-child problems, and other relational problems.

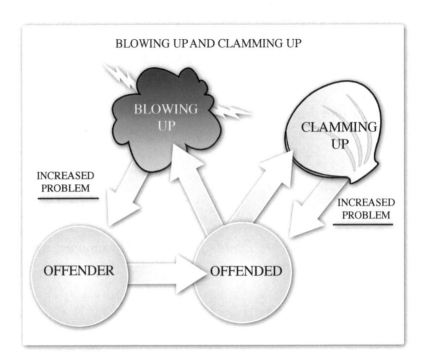

Anger is a sin that is a result of what we think, believe, or desire in our heart. It is an outpouring of the contents of the heart. It would be a fruit issue in a person's life. Galatians 5:20 lists anger, strife, disputes, dissentions, and enmity as deeds of the flesh. All of these are heart issues and are displayed as fruit in the life of the angry person. The Bible is clear on God's command to us to put away this destructive feeling and emotion on the heart level.

Anger is the manifestation of the problem or the fruit that is visible to the naked eye. A wise person will look beyond the fruit of anger to the root, or the heart of the problem.

Anger is an issue that flows out of the heart. It must be dealt with on the heart level. Any attempt to deal with only the results or the emotion of anger will be temporary and in the long run ineffective. We may have noticed this in prior attempts to deal with this problem.

To have long-term and even complete success, we really have to get at the roots of anger.

Let's examine what motivates and feeds anger.

Feelings of anger are generally (wrongly) handled in one of two ways: blowing up (screaming, ranting raving, hollering, hitting, breaking things, driving too fast or recklessly) or clamming up (quietly internalizing the emotions, seething). Those who clam up are more prone to depression.

In either case, this anger is usually self-centered and idolatrous and comes from wanting to control God but being unable to do so. Much of the problem of sinful anger stems from a desire to control people and circumstances.

Sinful anger and bitterness are the two most destructive emotions the human being possesses. Both are common problems in counseling. Because our new goal is to provoke a person to think instead of focus on how they feel, we have to teach the counselee how to do this.

These questions are intended to provoke thought, to expose what the person believes, and what they desire in their heart. When I am confronted by an angry counselee or person, I ask a series of questions like these you see before you. You may want to answer these for yourself so you are familiar with the struggles that people encounter as they train themselves to think versus feel.

Questions for the reader:
What did you want that you did not get?

What did you get that you did not want?

What do you believe would make you happy?

Do you believe you are entitled to be angry?

Do you think you have a right to be angry? (On what is that "right" based?)

Who do you believe is denying you these perceived rights?

Why do you believe you are entitled to these things? Can your "rights" be supported by Scripture?

Have you learned that you can justify your angry outbursts/actions?

For many angry people, their responses have become so habitual that they respond without much thought. The outburst of anger is something they just "do" such as breathing.

These questions are intended to reveal the heart and to provoke a person to think. Based on a person's answers to questions like those above, we can literally see where the sin is and then we can move on to how to correct it.

Asking questions is one way to engage the brain to think rather than to label everything a feeling. Asking questions also pricks the conscience and the response to my questions gives me the first opportunity to help them see the heart and mind renewal that is needed.

> Questions prick the conscience;
> Statements harden the heart.
> **Julie Ganschow**

To understand sinful anger, we have to look to the Scriptures to see what admonitions and commands God has for us regarding it.

> *Let all bitterness and wrath and anger and clamor and slander be put away from you, along with all malice.* **Ephesians 4:31 (NASB)**

> *But now you also, put them all aside: anger, wrath, malice, slander, and abusive speech from your mouth.* **Colossians 3:8 (NASB)**

> *My dear brothers, take note of this: Everyone should be quick to listen, slow to speak and slow to become angry, for man's anger does not bring about the righteous life that God desires.* **James 1:19-20 (NIV)**

> *Don't say, "I will get even for this wrong." Wait for the LORD to handle the matter.* **Proverbs 20:22 (NLT)**

These are not mere suggestions; these are commands from a holy God! Anger is a sin that leads to other sins including wrath, envy, jealousy, and murder. Put these things away from you!

God does not want us using the emotion He gave us for sinful purposes. We must understand that continuing to practice angry living and unbiblical methods for dealing with anger will be further living in idolatry of self.

Habitual anger is a manifestation (fruit) of idolatry. It is the fruit or product of living for self.

The angry person will not tolerate being denied his own way, or having his plan thwarted without an angry response. He believes that everyone and everything

should cater to him or please him. He, in essence, is placing himself in the role and position of a god.

This is in contrast to and in conflict with what the Bible says.

> *You shall have no other gods before Me.*   **Exodus 20:3 (NLT)**

The focus of the angry person is on self - not others, and not God. This is why habitual anger, whether demonstrated by blowing up or clamming up, is idolatry.

Questions for the reader:
Have you ever thought of anger as idolatry?

Overcoming Sinful Anger Biblically

Once we understand that sinful anger is the result of idolatry in the heart, we can begin to address the problem. We can learn how to overcome this bad habit. The object of heart worship must change from self to God.

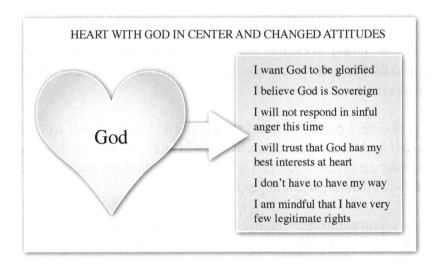

HEART WITH GOD IN CENTER AND CHANGED ATTITUDES

God

I want God to be glorified

I believe God is Sovereign

I will not respond in sinful anger this time

I will trust that God has my best interests at heart

I don't have to have my way

I am mindful that I have very few legitimate rights

This requires that we tell ourselves no, it is not alright to sin in my anger; no, it is not alright to consider myself so highly. We must begin to demonstrate self-control in our daily lives.

Scripture tells us:

> *Do not let sin control the way you live; do not give in to its lustful desires. Do not let any part of your body become a tool of wickedness, to be used for sinning. Instead, give yourselves completely to God since you have been given new life. And use your whole body as a tool to do what is right for the glory of God.* **Romans 6:12-13 (NLT)**

When we sin in our anger, we use our bodies as tools of wickedness - whether it is the tongue, or the hands, or the mind.

Review Romans 6 and see how Paul is speaking from the perspective of victory. This should give us hope! We are enabled to "give ourselves completely to God" because of Christ. In essence, He is saying now that you are enabled to do what is right, DO IT!

A new response to anger is difficult but not impossible for the one who has the victory in Christ. Christ is the way out! We are all able, through the power of the Holy Spirit, to deny ourselves and learn to respond differently.

There will indeed be struggles as a person wrestles with their thoughts, desires, and emotions. The angry person has learned a pattern of response, and it may be a long-standing habit. It may take some time for them to retrain themselves, but we must encourage them because we have hope - the believer has a mighty Advocate!

Immediate change can be seen in a person's life but not by following a program of steps to overcome anger. We can certainly offer helpful suggestions, but we are not interested in only changing behavior! The goal is to reach the **heart** of both the one who blows up and the one who clams up so that Jesus can change it. We have no power to change anyone. Our goal is to be pointing people toward Christ for He is the One who changes hearts and minds and lives and sets the captives free!

To effect change, a person must fill the mind with Scripture that will help them become self-controlled when tempted to sin in anger. A new mindset that is biblically oriented must be developed so that the new thinking becomes the default position rather than the usual angry responses.

One who is tempted to blow up must train themselves to apply the emotion of anger toward fixing or addressing the problem. One who is tempted to stuff or clam up the anger must learn to appropriately verbalize what caused the anger and then take steps to correct the problem.

Questions for the reader:

How do these attitudes toward anger differ from what you have heard before?

How does this differ from the popular "anger management" techniques?

The major important weapon in our arsenal against sinful anger is to learn about the sovereignty of God. As we learn about His sovereignty, it will revolutionize our thinking. When we are able to see the problems and frustrations of life from His perspective, they take on an entirely different hue. We can then see God's hand working and moving in each situation. Having our own way will no longer be as important to us because we will see things from His eyes. This is an important step in removing self from the center of the universe.

These verses reveal God's mind on those who refuse to accept His sovereign will.

> *But who are you, O man, to talk back to God? Shall what is formed say to him who formed it, "Why did you make me like this?"*
> **Romans 9:20 (NIV)**

> *Who is this that questions my wisdom with such ignorant words?*
> **Job 38:2 (NLT)**

> *Then the LORD said to Job, "Do you still want to argue with the Almighty? You are God's critic, but do you have the answers?"*
> **Job 40:1-2 (NLT)**

> *The earth is the LORD'S, and everything in it. The world and all its people belong to him.*
> **Psalm 24:1 (NLT)**

> *I, the LORD, search all hearts and examine secret motives. I give all people their due rewards, according to what their actions deserve.*
> **Jeremiah 17:10 (NLT)**

Chapter Nine

Understanding the Sovereignty of God

Question(s) for the reader:
How do you react when adversity or serious trials come your way?

Briefly describe one of the most troubling times you have experienced.

In your trouble, did you find yourself asking God, "Why is this happening to me?"

Were you angry at God for the trouble (would you admit you were angry with God for allowing the trouble)?

Do you ever think that God makes mistakes?

Did you complain that life was not fair when the trouble came?

Did you feel sorry for yourself?

Did you actively trust God in your troubles? How?

These questions are all related to God's sovereignty—a vastly misunderstood doctrine and therefore, virtually ignored by many Christians when trouble comes.

Dr. Jay Adams explains how the gaps in our theology of God have a direct bearing on how we react when trouble comes:

When trouble comes, many Christians react in ways that reflect the fundamentally non-Christian views still too much part of their lives. Were you to ask them, in a purely academic setting, whether God is involved in their trouble, doubtless they would affirm He is. But when push comes to shove, and they are faced with a devastating trial of one sort or another, their working atheism (or, at best deism) rises to the surface. All the rhetorical "whys," the bitter complaints, the hand-wringing self-pity, the seething anger, and the coming apart at the seams demonstrates a focus on self that effectively excludes God, at least for the moment.[1]

Jay Adams

Adams states that for many of us when an emotionally troubling crisis comes our way, our God and His involvement in our lives becomes an abstraction, or as Adams calls it, a working atheism. This is particularly true in a culture that is highly psychologized and fosters the thinking that God is responsible for the relatively good things in life but not involved in the relatively bad things. There are, perhaps, hundreds of passages in Scripture that attest to God's absolute sovereignty in the affairs of men; perhaps, the best example could be drawn from the book of Job. (Read through Job 1-2 at this time.)

> *There was a man in the land of Uz whose name was Job; and that man was blameless, upright, fearing God and turning away from evil.*
>
> **Job 1:1 (NASB)**

The very first verse in the book of Job tells us that Job was a man who trusted God (feared God) and that while not perfect (Rom. 3:23), he walked in a consistent, blameless manner. The verse sets the stage to help us understand that sometimes bad things happen to relatively good people, and they are not necessarily punishment from God as Job's so-called friends would later suggest.

Questions for the reader:

Think about a time when you experienced the loss of a loved one or a significant loss of property or possessions. Describe the situation and your emotions.

Seven sons and three daughters were born to him. His possessions also were 7,000 sheep, 3,000 camels, 500 yoke of oxen, 500 female donkeys, and very many servants; and that man was the greatest of all the men of the east.   **Job 1:2-3 (NASB)**

Job was blessed with ten children and with great wealth. Verses 4-5 indicate that Job cared for his family by offering sacrifices to God in case any of them sinned against God. We see here a man who takes his relationship with God very seriously; and it amazes us all the more by what comes next because for many of us, we attribute blessings as coming from God, but not hardship.

From the following verses (6-12) we see that God allows Satan to test Job. The tests are severe (13-19), and Job loses all of his children and all of his wealth.

Questions for the reader:

Who was directly responsible for Job's losses? (See verse 1:12 for a reminder)

Who did Job believe to be indirectly responsible? (See verse 1:21)

What was Job's response to his losses? (See verse 1:22)

Through all this, Job did not sin nor did he blame God.
Job 1:22 (NASB)

To not blame God means to not charge God with any wrongdoing. Dr. John MacArthur explains:

> Hasty words against God in the midst of grief are foolish and wicked. Christians are to submit to trials and still worship God, not because they see the reasons for them, but because God wills them and has His own reasons which believers are to trust.[2]
>
> **John MacArthur**

Job grieved the loss of his family. Of course, this is not sin, and even Jesus grieved the loss of his friend (John. 11:35). Yet, in his extreme grief, Job did not come apart at the seams and become a functional atheist. He did not understand the reasons for these calamities, but he trusted God in them. But, the story gets worse before it gets better.

Again Satan petitions God (Job 2:1-8), and God grants that Satan may test Job yet again; this time by afflicting his health! Job was smitten with a terrible illness; he was literally covered with painful boils in a day and age when there was little to no medicinal remedies. Even Job's wife had had enough and encouraged Job to turn his back on God.

> *Then his wife said to him, "Do you still hold fast your integrity? Curse God and die!"* **Job 2:9 (NASB)**

Job's response is remarkable:

> *But he said to her, "You speak as one of the foolish women speaks. Shall we indeed accept good from God and not accept adversity?" In all this Job did not sin with his lips.* **Job 2:10 (NASB)**

Questions for the reader:
From where does Job say come adversity (like sickness)?

Look up Amos 3:6. What does it say about the origin of disasters?

The evil Satan causes is only by the permission of God... It would be unbiblical and irrelevant to attribute to Satan (or sinful man) the power to frustrate the designs of God.[3] **John Piper**

The sovereignty of God is often questioned because man does not understand what God is doing. Because He does not act as we think He should, we conclude He cannot act as we think He would.[4] **Jerry Bridges**

In time, Job becomes worn out. His friends believe he is somehow responsible for his troubles because of some sin. The illness is painful, and his earlier submissiveness to God's secret will gives way to Job questioning God. From our side of reality, this seems quite normal and logical. In fact, I would say there is probably not a person reading this chapter who has not done exactly the same thing at one time or the other. We identify with Job because, after all, he is just asking God for an explanation.

> *Therefore I will not restrain my mouth; I will speak in the anguish of my spirit, I will complain in the bitterness of my soul.* **Job 7:11 (NASB)**

Again, we do not find it remarkable that Job begins to question God. What we do find remarkable is how God chooses to answer Job.

Then the LORD answered Job out of the whirlwind and said, *"Who is this that darkens counsel? By words without knowledge? Now gird up your loins like a man, And I will ask you, and you instruct Me! Where were you when I laid the foundation of the earth? Tell Me, if you have understanding."* (Job 38:1-4, NASB)

In the longest speech by God in the entire Bible (Job 38-41), God teaches Job about His absolute sovereignty to do as He wills. He explains all of Job's trials and troubles as the result of His absolute right to do with His creatures what He pleases.

Job does not react by declaring that God is unfair or unconcerned. Instead, Job repents, declaring that he was complaining about things he did not understand. (Job 42:3)

Questions for the reader:
Read Genesis 37-50 and the story of Joseph.

List Joseph's trials and troubles.

What does Joseph himself say about these things? (See Gen. 50:20)

Genesis 50:20 is sometimes called the Romans 8:28 of the Old Testament. Let's compare the two verses.

As for you, you meant evil against me, but God meant it for good in order to bring about this present result, to preserve many people alive.
Genesis 50:20 (NASB)

And we know that God causes all things to work together for good to those who love God, to those who are called according to His purpose.
Romans 8:28 (NASB)

Joseph's brothers meant evil against Joseph just as Satan sought to harm Job. God set limits as to how far Satan could go in that harm, and He set limits upon Joseph's brothers' schemes to harm him.

Joseph, like Job, understood God's sovereign control and His limitations on secondary causes such as Satan, the sins of people, and even natural disasters. In Joseph's case, we see that Joseph saw how God let things run their course-when he was in the pit, when he was falsely accused by Potiphar's wife, and when he was in prison for a crime he did not commit. This was to accomplish a greater goal that was invisible to Joseph. God used all of those circumstances behind the scenes to accomplish something that brings glory to Himself —the figurative salvation of many people who would starve without Joseph's inter-vention and forgiveness of his brothers.

To understand Romans 8:28, we must first understand that every book in the Bible is somehow about Christ and God's plan in redemptive history. With this is mind, we see that Joseph in many ways parallels Jesus Christ in the New Testament and serves as a type of Christ, that is, a type of Savior. This chart from the New American Standard Bible from Thomas Nelson Publishers illustrates the comparison. [5]

	Joseph A Type of Christ[5]	
Joseph	**Parallels**	**Jesus**
Gen 37:2	A shepherd of his father's sheep.	Jn 10:11, 27–29
Gen 37:3	His father loved him dearly.	Mt 3:17
Gen 37:4	Hated by his brothers.	Jn 7:4, 5
Gen 37:13, 14	Sent by father to brothers.	Heb 2:11
Gen 37:20	Others plotted to harm them.	Jn 11:53
Gen 37:23	Robes taken from them.	Jn 19:23, 24

	Joseph A Type of Christ	
Joseph	**Parallels**	**Jesus**
Gen 37:26	Taken to Egypt.	Mt 2:14, 15
Gen 37:28	Sold for the price of a slave.	Mt 26:15
Gen 39:7	Tempted.	Mt 4:1
Gen 39:16–18	Falsely accused.	Mt 26:59, 60
Gen 39:20	Bound in chains.	Mt 27:2
Gen 40:2, 3	Placed with two other prisoners, one who was saved and the other lost.	Lk 23:32
Gen 41:41	Exalted after suffering.	Php 2:9–11
Gen 41:46	Both 30 years old at the beginning of public recognition.	Lk 3:23
Gen 42:24; 45:2, 14, 15; 46:29	Both wept.	Jn 10:35
Gen 45:1–15	Forgave those who wronged them.	Lk 23:34
Gen 45:7	Saved their nation.	Mt 1:21
Gen 50:20	What men did to hurt them, God turned to good.	1Co 2:7, 8
	© 1997 by Thomas Nelson, Inc.	

In other words, in the story of Joseph, who saved his people from physical hunger, we see a picture of the coming Christ who would save His people from their spiritual poverty and hunger.

Romans 8:28 does not tell us that all things are good. It tells us that God uses all things for the good of those who love Him. While we, like Job and Joseph, often do not understand exactly how God does this one thing, we can be sure that He uses these things to help us become more like Christ.

> *And we know that God causes all things to work together for good to those who love God, to those who are called according to His purpose.*
> **Romans 8:28 (NASB)**

In the end, Job repented of questioning God. He was humble, thus reflecting the nature of Christ, who humbled Himself (Phil. 2:6-8) so that those who believe will be saved.

Joseph forgave those who sinned against him, thus reflecting the forgiveness of Christ when he died on the cross.

The doctrine of God's absolute sovereignty ought to be a great comfort to us because we know God is using all of our circumstances and all of our trials to help us become more like Christ in our responses to these troubles.

There is a promise in 1 Corinthians 10:13:

> *No temptation has overtaken you but such as is common to man; and God is faithful, who will not allow you to be tempted beyond what you are able, but with the temptation will provide the way of escape also, so that you will be able to endure it.* **1 Corinthians 10:13 (NASB)**

In the New Testament the same Greek word is used for both temptation and trial. God promises us that whatever the circumstance we need not sin in response to it. We will, by His grace, be able to endure it.

Once we understand that God is in absolute control of each and every situation, we can step out in faith and trust Him because God will allow nothing to detract from His glory. He will allow nothing to detract from the ultimate good of His people. Romans 8:28-29 is a promise. It's a promise that no matter what happens, we can be assured that God is working behind the scenes for the ultimate good for those that truly love Him. John MacArthur explains:

> In His providence, God orchestrates every event in life—even suffering, temptation, and sin—to accomplish both our temporal and eternal benefit (cf. Deut. 8:15, 16).[6] **John MacArthur**

This is why, when faced with adversity, our faith must triumph over our feelings. There is purpose in our adversities; while we may not totally understand the bigger picture, we can understand that God is using all things to make us more like Jesus.

> *For those whom He foreknew, He also predestined to become conformed to the image of His Son, so that He would be the firstborn among many brethren.* **Romans 8:29 (NASB)**

> All people—believers as well as unbelievers—experience anxiety, frustration, heartache and disappointment. Some suffer intense physical pain and catastrophic tragedies. But that which should distinguish the suffering of believers from unbelievers is the confidence that our suffering is under the control of an all powerful and all-loving God; our suffering has meaning and purpose in God's eternal plan, and He brings or allows to come into our lives only that which is for His glory and our good.[7] **Jerry Bridges**

105

When we are faced with adversity we are tempted to question God's wisdom. We wonder if somehow God is making a mistake. My son's best friend since the third grade was diagnosed with cancer. Fortunately, it was caught in time and he has made a full recovery. But my first thought upon receiving the news was, "Lord how can this be?" My son's friend is only 27 and in the prime of his life. He is married, and he and his bride just had their first baby. I asked, "Lord, how can this be?" thus questioning the Lord's wisdom. My emotional response cast doubt on God's wisdom, as well as His love, since my son's friend was (and is) a faithful believer.

The apostle Paul, in reflecting upon God's wisdom, exclaimed:

> *Oh, the depth of the riches both of the wisdom and knowledge of God!*
> *How unsearchable are His judgments and unfathomable His ways!*
> **Romans 11:33 (NASB)**

Paul means to say that we are limited in our understanding and our wisdom while God is not limited in any way. God sees the big picture while our view is limited to the here and now. J.I. Packer notes that wisdom is the practical side of moral goodness.[8] This means that God's wisdom goes hand-in-hand with God, always making the right call, the right decision—decisions that ultimately bring Him glory and for the benefit of His people.

> *Great is our Lord and abundant in strength; His understanding is infi-*
> *nite.* **Psalm 147:5 (NASB)**

God is not like us. He has full understanding of all the things we see as variables. He never second guesses a decision like we do. Here is where we struggle. We tend to see our lives as the center of all things and all things revolve around us and our personal happiness. Much of that is the result of how psychology has come to dominate us at the expense of sound theology. God always chooses the course of action that will ultimately bring Him the most glory. That notion runs contrary to the idea that everything is about me and the way I feel about things.

First Corinthians 10:31 exhorts us that in whatever we do, we do all for the glory of God. This is because God is most concerned for His own glory for the benefit of His people.

When we doubt God's goodness in our adversity and question His wisdom, we question His love for us. Therefore, Paul's words in Romans 8 seem meaningless.

> God never pursues His glory at the expense of the good of His people, nor does He ever seek our good at the expense of His glory. He has designed His eternal purpose so that His glory and our good are inextricably bound together. What comfort and encouragement this should be to us. If we are going to learn to trust God in adversity, we must believe that just as certainly as God will allow nothing to subvert His glory, so He will allow nothing to spoil the good He is working out in us and for us.[9]
> **Jerry Bridges**

> *Who will separate us from the love of Christ? Will tribulation, or distress, or persecution, or famine, or nakedness, or peril, or sword?...*
> *But in all these things we overwhelmingly conquer through Him who loved us.* **Romans 8:35, 37 (NASB)**

Paul knew something about adversity. He knew tribulation, distress, persecution, famine, nakedness, peril, and the threat of the sword, yet he believed we could conquer all these adversities through Christ. He believed this because the love of Christ was real to him and applicable in the midst of adversities.

The cross of Jesus Christ is never far from Paul's thinking. Paul never forgot the wonderment of the cross that Jesus Christ, in a supreme act of love, would die for Him. He counts everything as a loss compared to the wonderment of knowing Christ and Christ crucified:

> *Indeed, I count everything as loss because of the surpassing worth of knowing Christ Jesus my Lord. For his sake I have suffered the loss of all things and count them as rubbish, in order that I may gain Christ and be found in him, not having a righteousness of my own that comes from the law, but that which comes through faith in Christ, the righteousness from God that depends on faith— that I may know him and the power of his resurrection, and may share his sufferings, becoming like him in his death, that by any means possible I may attain the resurrection from the dead.* **Philippians 3:8-11 (ESV)**

The apostle John also reflected on the amazing love of God through Jesus and His death on the cross for our sins:

> *In this the love of God was made manifest among us, that God sent his only Son into the world, so that we might live through him. In this is love, not that we have loved God but that he loved us and sent his Son to be the propitiation for our sins.* **1 John 4:9-10 (ESV)**

Our greatest need is not to feel better about ourselves. It's not even the pursuit of happiness. Our greatest need is to be accepted as the beloved—that God would love us first in order that we love Him. If we think about all the possible adversities in life, all the potential calamities, they all pale in comparison to the terrible calamity of eternal separation from God. Consider Romans 5:8:

> *… but God shows his love for us in that while we were still sinners, Christ died for us.*   **Romans 5:8**
> **(ESV)**

While we were still sinners, still wretched, still self-centered, still miserable, still rebellious, and still bent on having our own way and pursuing our own happiness, Christ died for us.

How should this knowledge help us in our adversities? When we are tempted to doubt God's love, we need to return to the cross.

> We must not allow our emotions to hold sway over our minds. Our emotions must become subservient to the truth… If God's love was sufficient for my greatest need, my eternal salvation, surely it is sufficient for my lesser needs, the adversities I encounter in this life… This infinite, measureless love of God is poured out on us, not because of who we are or what we are, but because we are in Christ Jesus.[10]
>
> **Jerry Bridges**

For the Christian, the Lord Jesus Christ is our environment, an ever present help in times of trouble (Psa. 46:1). He is wisdom, He is sufficient, and He is our advocate and great high priest.

> *Since then we have a great high priest who has passed through the heavens, Jesus, the Son of God, let us hold fast our confession. For we do not have a high priest who is unable to sympathize with our weaknesses, but one who in every respect has been tempted as we are, yet without sin. Let us then with confidence draw near to the throne of grace, that we may receive mercy and find grace to help in time of need.*
> **Hebrews 4:14-16 (ESV)**

Chapter Ten

Understanding the Sufficiency of Christ[1]

> To encounter Christ is to touch reality and experience transcendence. He gives us a sense of self-worth or personal significance, because He assures us of God's love for us. He sets us free from guilt because He died for us... and from paralyzing fear because He reigns... He gives meaning to marriage and home, work and leisure, personhood and citizenship.[2]
>
> **John Stott**
>
> Do not tell me that there is no rest for us till we get to heaven. We who have believed in Jesus enter into rest even now. Why should we not do so? Our salvation is complete. The robe of righteousness in which we are clad is finished. The atonement for our sins is fully made. We are reconciled to God, beloved of the Father, preserved by His grace, and supplied by His providence with all that we need. We carry all our burdens to Him and leave them at His feet. We spend our lives in His service, and we find His ways to be ways of pleasantness, and His paths to be paths of peace. Oh, yes, we have found rest unto our souls! I recollect the first day that I ever rested in Christ, and I did rest that day. And so will all of you who trust in Jesus as I trusted in him.
>
> **C.H. Spurgeon**
>
> This explains why Christ is sometimes not enough for us. If I stand before him as a cup waiting to be filled with psychological satisfaction, I will never feel quite full. Why? First, because my lusts are boundless; by their very nature, they can't be filled. Second, because Jesus does not intend to satisfy my selfish desires. Instead, he intends to break the cup of psychological need (lusts), not fill it.[3]
>
> **Edward T. Welch**

The Insufficiency of Christ

> *See to it that no one takes you captive through philosophy and empty deception, according to the tradition of men, according to the elementary principles of the world, rather than according to Christ.*
>
> **Colossians 2:8 (NASB)**

Pastor-Teacher John MacArthur, in a sermon titled, "Jesus Plus Nothing Equals Everything," says:

> It seems to me that if I were not a Christian and if I were just out there living in the world, and some well-intentioned person approached me and asked if I would be interested in being a Christian, the first question that I would ask would be, "What does Christianity provide for me? What does Christianity offer?"[4]

I think what MacArthur means is this:

Have you ever seen the commercials that advertise for the military? Here are some of the slogans I found:

- "Be all you can be." (Marines)
- "Be an Army of one." (Army)
- "Accelerate your life." (Navy)
- "Get to where you want to go." (Air Force)

If a person, drawn in by the slogan, were to go see the recruiter, they might ask, "What does your service have to offer me?"

The recruiter would skillfully introduce them to the many opportunities their branch of the military offers in an effort to get them to enlist in their particular branch of service. The Marines market themselves as an elite fighting force that appeals in particular to young males. The Army is similar but tends to emphasize leadership skills that can be used after military service has ended. The Navy and Air Force emphasize the excitement of being around a lot of high-tech equipment.

A wise recruiter would gently probe what the potential recruit was interested in and sell him or her on the service as the best way for them to get what they wanted.

Now, let's imagine for a minute you are not a Christian and someone asked you if you were interested in becoming one. What might you logically say or ask?

You might say, "Why should I join up? What do you have to offer that another religion does not? What is in it for me if I commit to Christianity?"

What does Christianity offer may be a valid question to ask of the recruiter. The question is, what kind of answers are delivered by today's recruiters?

Some modern recruiters to Christianity might say that if you join up you will be healthy, wealthy and wise. Others might say that upon enlistment you will experience a sense of inner peace and tranquility. Still others would take you to the power of positive thinking or possibility thinking in your quest to become a better you and solve your problems.

Like a good military recruiter doing his job, a modern recruiter to Christianity might be tempted to tell the potential recruit what he thinks he or she wants to hear in order to sell the package and "close the deal."

If we are honest, we can mold this thing called Christianity into anything we would like it to be. We can sell it. We can market it. We can make people buy it if we correctly present the benefit that people want to hear.

110

The gospel in America has become highly psychologized. I would go so far as to say that the bulk of the church is in a type of "Babylonian Captivity" to Christianized Psychology, and that a psychologized message is what has grown churches.

Questions for the reader:

What did people do before the advent of psychology when they had personal problems of fear, worry, anxiety and depression and other common problems?

Be patient. Is God not fast enough? Are His answers too tough? A quick sympathy from a friend may suggest that you simply drop out, be good to yourself, get away from it all. Someone else will be sure to say, "You need counsel." Are you sure? One hour at the foot of the Cross may obviate the necessity of professional counseling (no such thing existed until the twentieth century – what did folks do before then?)[5]   **Elisabeth Elliot**

What Does Christianity Offer?

So, what does genuine Christianity offer? It offers Christ. It offers Christ crucified for the forgiveness of sins. Consider Scripture:

> *… but we preach Christ crucified, to Jews a stumbling block and to Gentiles foolishness.*   **1 Corinthians 1:23 (NASB)**

The preceding verse to 1 Corinthians 1:23 says the Greeks seek wisdom. Paul replies by saying that Christ is the only true wisdom to be had.

Instead of this plain, straight forward message, some apparently believe it is not enough and the message must be massaged to make it more palatable to unbelievers. Paul will have none of that.

> *For I delivered to you as of first importance what I also received, that Christ died for our sins according to the Scriptures.*   **1 Corinthians 15:3 (NASB)**

Preaching Christ crucified was of first importance to Paul because he realized that the response to his message provided the only real hope to those who heard him. Man's greatest need is not to feel good about himself, nor is it to take hold of the power of possibility thinking, nor is it to fulfill all his ambitions and desires. Man's greatest need is for a crucified Christ and to be satisfied in Him.

> Saving faith is the confidence that if you sell all you have, and forsake all sinful pleasures, the hidden treasure of holy joy will satisfy your deepest desires. Saving faith is the heartfelt conviction not only that Christ is reliable, but also that he is desirable. It is the confidence that he will come through with his promises and that what he promises is more to be desired than all the world.[6]
> **John Piper**

Paul was clear that knowing Christ was of surpassing value and that nothing else was needed:

> *But whatever things were gain to me, those things I have counted as loss for the sake of Christ. More than that, I count all things to be loss in view of the surpassing value of knowing Christ Jesus my Lord, for whom I have suffered the loss of all things, and count them but rubbish so that I may gain Christ, and may be found in Him, not having a righteousness of my own derived from the Law, but that which is through faith in Christ, the righteousness which comes from God on the basis of faith, that I may know Him and the power of His resurrection and the fellowship of His sufferings, being conformed to His death; in order that I may attain to the resurrection from the dead.* **Philippians 3:7-11 (NASB)**

Paul was also clear that those who have received Christ as Lord and Savior have many benefits in Him and that nothing needs to be added:

> *Blessed be the God and Father of our Lord Jesus Christ, who has blessed us with every spiritual blessing in the heavenly places in Christ.*
> **Ephesians 1:3 (NASB)**

> *God alone made it possible for you to be in Christ Jesus. For our benefit God made Christ to be wisdom itself. He is the one who made us acceptable to God. He made us pure and holy, and he gave himself to purchase our freedom.* **1 Corinthians 1:30 (NLT)**

Peter echoes Paul:

> *Seeing that His divine power has granted to us everything pertaining to life and godliness, through the true knowledge of Him who called us by His own glory and excellence. For by these He has granted to us His precious and magnificent promises, so that by them you may become*

partakers of the divine nature, having escaped the corruption that is in the world by lust. **2 Peter 1:3-4 (NASB)**

But Paul had a problem with the Colossian Church just as he did with the Galatians and Corinthians. Some were being led astray. They were losing their focus on the gospel and being led away from the first importance of knowing Christ and their sufficiency in Him.

> Without Christ you have nothing. With Christ you have everything.[7]
> **John MacArthur**

See to it that no one takes you captive through philosophy and empty deception, according to the tradition of men, according to the elementary principles of the world, rather than according to Christ. **Colossians 2:8 (NASB)**

O foolish Galatians! Who has bewitched you? It was before your eyes that Jesus Christ was publicly portrayed as crucified. Let me ask you only this: Did you receive the Spirit by works of the law or by hearing with faith? Are you so foolish? Having begun by the Spirit, are you now being perfected by the flesh? **Galatians 3:1-3 (ESV)**

I am jealous for you with a godly jealousy. I promised you to one husband, to Christ, so that I might present you as a pure virgin to him. But I am afraid that just as Eve was deceived by the serpent's cunning, your minds may somehow be led astray from your sincere and pure devotion to Christ. For if someone comes to you and preaches a Jesus other than the Jesus we preached, or if you receive a different spirit from the one you received, or a different gospel from the one you accepted, you put up with it easily enough. **2 Corinthians 11:2-4 (NIV)**

The point is we are easily led astray and like the Corinthians, "put up with it easily enough."

> We have only one message, and that is Christ. We tell sinners they can have a relationship with Christ and in that relationship with Him, they will receive everything they need, all spiritual blessings in the heavenlies. And yet in the name of Christianity, in the name of the gospel, in the name of the church, in the name of evangelism, people are told all kinds of things, promised all kinds of things, sold all kinds of things and in the middle somewhere is, if recognizable, a significantly diminished Christ. Anything that diminishes Jesus Christ is a perverted presentation, it is another gospel, a false gospel.[8]
> **John MacArthur**

113

Psychology

As I stated earlier, the church has been taken captive by the church growth movement's ability to market the gospel and sell a psychologized gospel. The result of people "putting up with it easily enough" has been an insufficient gospel and an insufficient Christ when it comes to dealing with the problems in daily living.

The fact is everyone is a theologian; even an atheist has a theology. His theological premise is God does not exist. This amounts to a teaching about God and is, therefore, a type of theology.

I did not say that everyone is a good theologian, only that we all have a philosophy or theology regarding God. It may be accurate, inaccurate, scriptural, sort of scriptural, or not scriptural at all, but we all have one.

So it is with Christian psychology. Christian psychology has to a lesser or greater extent been influenced by atheistic or non-believing psychiatrists. Christian psychology tends to look at theology or Scripture through the eclectic[9] lens of their profession rather than looking at psychology through the sound interpretation of Scripture.

Following are some of the non-Christian influences that have influenced Christian psychology.

Sigmund Freud

In Freudian psychology, man is not responsible for what he does. If that particular notion does not fill our culture's mind, I don't know what does. Nevertheless, Freud believed that our problems were because our evolutionary instincts were thwarted by the constraints of society, friends, family, and, of course, religion.

Freud taught that the cure for our problems was to follow our instincts and throw off the constraints. This sounds a lot like "if it feels good do it." Freud said that the liberation of self would bring happiness.

Of course, this brief description is contrary to biblical teaching. The Bible says we are responsible. We are guilty before a holy God for breaking His law and rebelling against Him. The Bible teaches that the solution to this problem is found in Jesus Christ and not in the liberation of self.

Carl Rogers

In Rogerian psychology, man's basic nature is good at the core of his being. Our problem is that our minds are blocked by negative thinking or influences and so

we do bad things or make mistakes. In Rogerian psychology, it's not really about sin and salvation it is about removing the negativity or influences.

This may be the dominate psychology / theology in the church today. Man is basically good and all we really need is a good course in self-improvement. We don't really need a Savior; instead we need a therapist to help us feel good about our inherent goodness. Rogerian psychology and its variants would be responsible for the over-emphasis on self-esteem and self-worth that comes from so many pulpits.

Rogerian teaching maintains that we have the answers inside of ourselves and all we need to do is tap into them. We need to release our inner potential and, as the Marines say, "Be all you can be."

The Bible, of course, does not say this. The Bible says our hearts are desperately wicked (Jer. 17:9) and that we do not know just how wicked they are! The Bible indicates that we are fully capable of even the worst of sins. Watching the nightly news is ample proof of that. The Bible teaches not that the answers are inside of us, but that the answers are found only in Christ.

Scripture teaches we desperately need a heart change and God the Holy Spirit to convict us of our sin.

> If Christ has died for me - ungodly as I am, without strength as I am -then I can no longer live in sin, but must arouse myself to love and serve Him who has redeemed me. I cannot trifle with the evil that killed my best Friend. I must be holy for His sake. How can I live in sin when He has died to save me from it?
> **C.H. Spurgeon**

B.F. Skinner

B.F. Skinner was another highly influential individual in American psychology. Skinner taught the behaviorist view that man is a highly evolved animal that could be trained with positive and negative stimuli. Skinner maintained our problems come from our environment and circumstances or things that happen to us. Skinner said that reprogramming from negative to positive could fix the problems.

Scripture does not teach macro-evolution (that man is a highly-evolved bag of random chemicals thrown together by chance). Scripture teaches that man is a special, unique creation with a soul, but that man fell and fell hard. As a result, creation itself is under a curse.

Man needs something more than reprogramming. He needs a new Adam who is the Christ to change his rebellious ways and disobedient heart so that he can respond to sovereignly ordained circumstances in order to bring glory to his Savior.

The Sufficiency of Christ

A dog barks when his master is attacked. I would be a coward if I saw that God's truth is attacked and yet would remain silent.   **John Calvin**

Truth always carries with it confrontation. Truth demands confrontation; loving confrontation nevertheless. If our reflex action is always accommodation regardless of the centrality of the truth involved, there is something wrong.   **Francis Schaeffer**

Upholding Truth, Undermining Falsehood

See to it that no one takes you captive through philosophy and empty deception, according to the tradition of men, according to the elementary principles of the world, rather than according to Christ.
Colossians 2:8 (NASB)

Paul, the great defender of the gospel truth, is warning against falsehood in Colossians 2:8-15. To better understand the warning, let's briefly examine the first seven verses of the chapter.

For I want you to know how great a struggle I have on your behalf and for those who are at Laodicea, and for all those who have not personally seen my face, that their hearts may be encouraged, having been knit together in love, and attaining to all the wealth that comes from the full assurance of understanding, resulting in a true knowledge of God's mystery, that is, Christ Himself, in whom are hidden all the treasures of wisdom and knowledge. I say this so that no one will delude you with persuasive argument. For even though I am absent in body, nevertheless I am with you in spirit, rejoicing to see your good discipline and the stability of your faith in Christ. Therefore as you have received Christ Jesus the Lord, so walk in Him, having been firmly rooted and now being built up in Him and established in your faith, just as you were instructed, and overflowing with gratitude.   **Colossians 2:1-7 (NASB)**

Paul is exhorting two main things in these seven verses:

1. Maintain allegiance to the deity of Christ. The early Gnostics were disputing the deity of Christ and some of the Colossians may have been falling into the same belief.
2. Paul is emphasizing our **complete sufficiency** in Him.

Paul begins the chapter with affirming some wonderful positives (vs 1-7) before he attacks serious error (vs 8-22).

While Paul is upholding truth and undermining error, he is a bit vague as to the exact nature of the error.

> When he now reaches the very heart of his letter the apostle dwells so eloquently upon the deity of Christ and the dignity and completeness of believers that the reader is left in some uncertainty as to the exact system of error against which the Colossians were to be upon their guard.[10]
> **Charles Erdman**

Paul's point seems to be that any false system will collapse if we know and embrace the truth. Let's examine Paul's main point in some detail.

> *See to it that no one takes you captive through philosophy and empty deception, according to the tradition of men, according to the elementary principles of the world, rather than according to Christ.*
> **Colossians 2:8 (NASB)**

See to it...

"See to it" is a phrase of emphasis, an imperative or command, an expectation that the Colossians act on his instructions. Having found freedom in Christ, see to it that you don't slip back into Christ plus something else.

Scripture is populated with warnings of error and exhortations to avoid wrong teaching:

- *Beware of false prophets…* (Matt. 7:15)
- *Watch out for the teaching of the Pharisees…* (Matt. 16:6)
- *Be on the alert for savage wolves…* (Acts 20:29-31)
- *Be aware of the dogs…* (Phil. 3:2)
- *Don't be carried away by false teaching…* (2 Pe. 3:1)

In fact, it is fair to say that much of the New Testament is dedicated to upholding truth and negating error in the Doctrine of Salvation and the Doctrine of Progressive Sanctification—two closely related doctrines.

See to it that no one takes you captive...

"See to it that no one takes you captive" is a word picture that means being taken captive in the sense of being kidnapped, or carried off as booty in the spoils of war.

> To Paul, it was unthinkable that those who had been ransomed and re-deemed should be vulnerable by ignorance and thus in the spiritual war become prisoners of some spiritual predator with false doctrine.[11]
> **John MacArthur**

It grieves us when we have to minister to someone taken captive by theology that is in deep error. What we believe has a direct bearing on how we live. So, it is a blessing when we can help them see the error, but it is quite sad when they do not realize they have been kidnapped and carried away by doctrines that threaten the gospel itself and are tragically content to remain in the error.

See to it that no one takes you captive through philosophy and empty deception...

Broadly speaking, philosophy means to love wisdom. Its usage here, though, is much broader than loving philosophy as an academic discipline. John MacArthur notes the term is broad enough to cover religious sects and, more importantly, the beliefs sects and cults hold in error.

Deception means "a deceit, fraud, or trick."[12]

The psychologized gospel is easy on the ears. The message revolves around the person's sense of self-worth or how to be a better you. Ironically, pulpits that preach a psychologized gospel are frequently quite large.

This does not mean that every man who preaches a psychologized gospel does so for church growth purposes. Nevertheless, a message that is about being a better you or designed to inflate your self-esteem is not the gospel, it is something else—a deceit, fraud, or trick. Millions of professing Christians do not know any better because they have not been taught how to discern truth from error.

Falsehood, to be effective, has to have a seducing effect. Man is basically good. It's not your fault. Release your inner self. Feel good about you. Words that communicate these things have a seducing effect—the words are easy on the ears and we want to hear things like this. Throw in some Scripture out of context and you have a very seducing message. Perhaps this is why Paul tells the Corinthians (2 Cor. 11:4) that they put up with another gospel quite easily enough.

Paul says it's an illusion, and it is.

See to it that no one takes you captive through philosophy and empty deception, according to the tradition of men…

Christian psychiatrists and psychologists have much training. Psychiatrists are also medical doctors and spend many years in training. Psychologists and associated professions with a strong psychology component are almost always trained through the master degree level. It adds up to many hours studying the subject and doing the work to earn such a degree.

It is then difficult for many of these men and women who have worked so hard in their chosen fields to hear that Christ is sufficient or His Word is sufficient for all the problems they have been trained to handle. It is understandable that they might take offense when one suggests to them their interpretation of Scripture is flawed, based more on the traditions of men rather than sound exegesis (exegesis means to interpret the text). To better understand this key point of Christian Psychiatry and Psychology (reading Scripture according to the traditions of men), let's look at this quote by John MacArthur:

> Most Christian psychologists view the Bible as an inspirational resource, but their basic system of counseling, both theory and methods, is transferred unaltered from secular psychology. Most are frankly and self-consciously eclectic, picking and choosing theories and techniques according to personal preference. In contrast, biblical counselors follow the Bible's view of itself as the source of a comprehensive and detailed approach to understanding and counseling people (2 Tim. 3:15–17; 2 Pet. 1:4).
>
> Some Christian psychotherapists use few Scriptures; others use many. But frequency of citation is much less important than the way passages are used—or misused—and in the vast majority of cases the passages cited are completely misused. There is a dearth of contextualized exegesis (a critical interpretation of a text) and an abundance of eisegesis (interpreting a text by reading one's own ideas into it). Biblical counseling is committed to letting God speak for Himself through His Word, and to handling the Word of Truth rightly (2 Tim. 2:15).[13]

It is easy to read into Scripture what you want it to say. It is easy to read into Scripture through the lens of psychology and, as the quotation says, this amounts to not letting God speak for Himself through His Word.

Since Freud, the study of psychology has produced a significant amount of tradition(s) that have been handed down as truth and/or scientific truth. Paul warns the Colossians to not be taken in by these kinds of traditions of men when they do not line up with Scripture. Paul writes to Timothy:

Do your best to present yourself to God as one approved, a worker who has no need to be ashamed, rightly handling the word of truth.

2 Timothy 2:15 (ESV)

See to it that no one takes you captive through philosophy and empty deception, according to the tradition of men, according to the elementary principles of the world, rather than according to Christ.

The phrase *elementary principles of the world* is difficult to interpret, so some caution is in order. *Elementary* seems to refer to the basics. It literally means the letters of the alphabet. Our children learn the basics, the alphabet, while they are in elementary school.

Therefore, it seems that Paul is telling the Colossians they are sufficient in Christ and they should not be distracted by worldly things.

Paul is saying that you have Christ, so why bother with this nonsense which is not in according with who you are in Christ?

An All Sufficient Christ

It is either all of Christ or none of Christ! I believe we need to preach again a whole Christ to the world - a Christ who does not need our apologies, a Christ who will not be divided, a Christ who will either be Lord of all or will not be Lord at all!
A.W. Tozer

*See to it that no one takes you captive through philosophy and empty deception, according to the tradition of men, according to the elementary principles of the world, rather than according to Christ. For **in Him** all the fullness of Deity dwells in bodily form, and **in Him** you have been made complete, and He is the head over all rule and authority; and **in Him** you were also circumcised with a circumcision made without hands, in the removal of the body of the flesh by the circumcision of Christ; having been buried **with Him** in baptism, in which you were also raised up **with Him** through faith in the working of God, who raised Him from the dead. When you were dead in your transgressions and the uncircumcision of your flesh, He made you alive together with Him, having forgiven us all our transgressions, having canceled out the certificate of debt consisting of decrees against us, which was hostile to us; and He has taken it out of the way, having nailed it to the cross. When He had disarmed the rulers and authorities, He made a public display of them, having triumphed over them **through Him.***

Colossians 2:8-15 (NASB)

I think that most of our problems in daily life stem from the fact we seem to have lost our vision for God. Perhaps it is because the psychologized gospel has become so popular we now have a much lower view of God and Christ than we once did. John MacArthur notes:

> Once we lose our vision for God, who He is, what He has done through His Son Jesus Christ, we get a vision for something else. God is put on the shelf, an abstraction. Christ's work on the Cross, a footnote in history that has application when I die but is irrelevant now.[14]

With such a low view of God, it is not surprising that people chase after additions to Christ—the empty philosophies, the traditions of men, having a form of godliness but lacking power (2 Tim. 3:5), because the power of God is denied in practice.

But Paul reminds us that we are "with Him" and "in Him." We are complete in Him, needing nothing else.

To be complete in Christ means to be positionally secure. God loves His saints the same yesterday, today, and tomorrow. We cannot add to grace nor can we subtract from grace by our performance.

We have the imputed righteousness of Christ. Imputed means *instead of*. It is not a righteousness of our own because we do not have any. We become the righteousness of God by trusting in Christ and His finished work on the cross.

> *He made Him who knew no sin to be sin on our behalf, so that we might become the righteousness of God in Him.*   **2 Corinthians 5:21 (NASB)**

God so loved the world that He sent His son to die for the many who would be "In Him." How indeed should this matter in our daily lives? Did God merely save us by the sufficiency of Christ's sacrifice only to allow us to get through life with something else plus Christ?

Questions for the reader:
With the help of a concordance, see how many times you can find the phase "in Him" in your New Testament.

How often to do you reflect on the meaning of being "in Him?"

121

Is there scriptural evidence that indicates that God has given us everything we need in Christ for the problems of daily living? Yes, there is.

> *Seeing that His divine power has granted to us everything pertaining to life and godliness, through the true knowledge of Him who called us by His own glory and excellence. For by these He has granted to us His precious and magnificent promises, so that by them you may become partakers of the divine nature, having escaped the corruption that is in the world by lust.* **2 Peter 1:3-4 (NASB)**

What does "His divine power" mean?
- Jesus Christ is the "power source" of the believer's sufficiency and perseverance.
- The Christian will persevere and grow in his or her faith because they have received all that is necessary to sustain eternal life through Christ's power.

Consider the commentary of John MacArthur again:

> To be godly is to live reverently, loyally, and obediently toward God. Peter means that the genuine believer ought not to ask God for something more (as if something necessary to sustain his growth, strength, and perseverance was missing) to become godly, because he already has every spiritual resource to manifest, sustain, and perfect godly living.[15]

The question then is one of belief. Do we really believe God has given us all we need to grow or mature in Christ?

Questions(s) for the reader:
Having come this far in our study of heart change, are you starting to realize the difference between living by faith and living by feelings?

In our *"in Him"* relationship with Christ, we have the means to access all the power we need to walk in the newness of life we received when we were born again.

> *What shall we say then? Are we to continue in sin so that grace may increase? May it never be! How shall we who died to sin still live in it? Or do you not know that all of us who have been baptized into Christ Jesus have been baptized into His death? Therefore we have been buried with Him through baptism into death, so that as Christ was raised from the dead through the glory of the Father, so we too might walk in newness of life.* **Romans 6:1-4 (NASB)**

God saved us to change us—to change us from sinners without hope to a newness in Christ with the power to become more like Christ. The same power that was used to raise Christ from the dead is available to make us more like Him.

God saved us to be in Jesus to become like Jesus.

Endnotes:

Preface

1. Observation made in Jim Owen's, *Christian Psychology's War on God's Word*, The Victimization of the Believer.
2. *Enhanced Strong's Lexicon* 5590, Electronic Ed., Libronix.
3. Owen, Jim. *Christian Psychology's War on God's Word*, (Santa Clara: East-Gate Publishers, 1993) 15.
4. Ibid, 17.

Chapter 1

1. Smith, Winston. Dichotomy or Trichotomy? How the Doctrine of Man Shapes the Treatment of Depression, *The Journal of Biblical Counseling*, (Vol. 18, Number 3, Spring 2000) 22
2. *Enhanced Strong's Lexicon 5590*, Electronic Ed., Libronix.
3. Adams, Jay E. *A Theology of Christian Counseling,* (Zondervan: Grand Rapids, 1979) 112.
4. MacArthur, John. *The MacArthur Study Bible* (electronic ed.) (Nashville, Word Publishing, 1997).
5. Bridges, Jerry. *The Practice of Godliness* (NavPress, 1996) 124.
6. MacArthur, *Study Bible*
7. Smith, "Trichotomy or Dichotomy?" 23
8. Adams, *Theology of Christian Counseling*, 110.
9. http://biblestudytools.net/lexicons/greek
10. Elliot, Elisabeth. *The Glad Surrender*, (Revell, 1982) 19–20.

Chapter 2

1. Peace, Martha. *Attitudes of a Transformed Heart* (Focus Publishing, 2002) 41.
2. Kaiser, Walter. *Toward an Exegetical Theology* (Baker, 1981) 7-8.
3. Grudem, Wayne. *Systematic Theology* (Zondervan, 1994).
4. Eyrich, Howard and William Hines. *Curing the Heart—A Model for Biblical Counseling* (Rossshire, UK: Christian Focus Publications LTD) 46.
5. MacArthur, John. *The Battle for the Beginning* (Thomas Nelson, 2001) 197.

Chapter 3

1. Boice, James Montgomery. *Romans, Vol I* (Grand Rapids, MI: Baker Book House, 1991) p.380, 447. Cited in *This Great Salvation, Unmerited Favor-Unmatched Joy*, by C.J. Mahaney and Robin Boisvert.

2. Ryken, Philip Graham. *Is Jesus the Only Way?* (Crossway, 1999) 41.
3. Mahaney, C.J. *Living the Cross Centered Life* (Multnomah Books a division of Random House, Copyright, Sovereign Grace Ministries, 2006) 13-4.

Chapter 4

1. Bridges, Jerry. *Respectable Sins*, (NavPress, 2007) 23.
2. Ibid, 25.
3. Piper, John. *The Blazing Center – The Soul Satisfying Supremacy of God in All Things*, Q&A, 2005.
4. Packer, James. *Your Father Loves You*, (Harold Shaw Publishers, 1986), page for April 17.
5. Mahaney, C.J. *The Idol Factory*, (Sovereign Grace Ministries, Gaithersburg, MD 20877).
www.sovereigngraceministries.org

Chapter 5

1. Welch, Edward T. *When People are Big and God is Small*, (P&R Publishing, 1997) 150.
2. *Strong's Hebrew and Greek Dictionaries Electronic Edition* © 1998, Parsons Technology, Inc.
3. Bridges, Jerry. *Trusting God*, (Navpress: 1988) 197.
4. Bridges, Jerry. *Transforming Grace*, (NavPress, 1991) 144.
5. Citation: sermon, Calvary Baptist Church, Newport, NJ (based on Rom.12:1-2) http://home.comcast.net/~pastorbob/sundaymorningsermons/romans/romans1212pt2.htm

Chapter 6

1. Piper, John. *How the Spirit Helps Us Understand, 1 Corinthians 2:14-16*, May 20, 1984. www.desiringGod.org.
2. Sande, Ken. *The Peacemaker* (Grand Rapids: Baker Books, 2004) 105.
3. Elliot, Elisabeth. *Discipline – The Glad Surrender*, (Revell, 1982) 69.
4. Bridges, Jerry. *Trusting God*, 37.

Chapter 7

1. MacArthur, John. *1 Corinthians*, (Chicago Moody Press, 1984) 147.
2. Piper, John. *Desiring God*, (Multnomah Books, 1996) 91.

Notes

Chapter 8

1. Mack, Wayne. *A homework Manual for Biblical Counselors, Vol 1I* (Phillipsburg, NJ: Presbyterian and Reformed Publishing Co).
2. Bridges, Jerry. *The Practice of Godliness*, (NavPress, 1996) 141.

Chapter 9

1. Adams, Jay E. *How To Handle Trouble* (Phillipsburg: Presbyterian and Reformed Publishing Co. 1982) 17.
2. MacArthur, *The MacArthur Study Bible*, Job 1:22.
3. Piper, *Desiring God*, 36.
4. Bridges, *Trusting God*, 22.
5. Chart in the New American Standard Bible—1995 update, Electronic version, copyright by Thomas Nelson, 1997.
6. *MacArthur Study Bible*, Rom. 8:28 notation, Thomas Nelson Electronic Edition, 1987.
7. Bridges, *Trusting God*, 32.
8. Packer, JI. *Knowing God*, (Downers Grove, IL: Intervarsity Press, 1973) 80.
9. Bridges, *Trusting God*, 25.
10. Bridges, *Trusting God*,140–2.

Chapter 10

1. The material in Chapter Ten was originally presented in sermon and teaching form at Grace Community Church, West Allis, WI by Pastor Bruce Roeder.
2. Stott, John. *Between Two Worlds* (Wm. B. Eerdmans Publishing Co., 1982), 154.
3. Welch, *When People are Big*, 149.
4. MacArthur, John. *Jesus Plus Nothing Equals Everything* (http://www.biblebb.com/).
5. Elliot, Elisabeth. *Secure in the Everlasting Arms* (Revell, 2002) 127.
6. Piper, *Desiring God*, 68.
7. MacArthur, *Jesus Plus Nothing*
8. MacArthur, John. *The Sufficiency of Christ Alone* (http://www.biblebb.com/).
9. Eclectic: 1) selecting or choosing from various sources, 2) made up of what is selected from different sources, 3) not following any one system, as of philosophy, medicine, etc., but selecting and using what are considered the best elements of all systems. http://dictionary.reference.com/browse/eclectic.
10. Erdman, Charles R. *The Epistles of Paul to the Colossians and to Philemon* (Philadelphia: Westminster, 1956) 73.
11. MacArthur, John. *The MacArthur New Testament Commentary on Colossians and Philemon* (Chicago: Moody Bible Institute, 1992) 99
12. Ibid, 99.
13. Ibid, 99.

14. MacArthur, Jr, John and Wayne A. Mack. Master's College: *Introduction to Biblical Counseling: Basic Guide to the Principles and Practice of Counseling.* Electronic ed. (Dallas, TX : Word Pub., 1997, c1994) 363.

15. MacArthur, *The MacArthur New Testament*, 99.

About the Authors

Julie Ganschow

Julie Ganschow has been involved in Biblical Counseling and Discipleship for more than 20 years. She is passionate about the critical need for heart change in a person who desires change in their life.

She is the founder and Director of Reigning Grace Counseling Center (ACBC, IABC Certified) and operates Biblical Counseling for Women. She has been writing a daily blog on counseling issues women face since 2008.

Her extensive training has led to a Master of Arts in Biblical Counseling and certification with the Association of Certified Biblical Counselors (ACBC) and the International Association of Biblical Counselors (IABC).

Julie is a gifted counselor and teacher and has authored numerous books and materials for biblical counseling and training. She is also a featured contributor in GriefShare and a frequent retreat and conference speaker.

She makes her home in Kansas City, MO. with her wonderful husband Larry. Their three sons are grown and married, and she is currently delighting in her grand babies.

You can find her blog at bc4women.org, and information about her ministries at www.rgcconline.org, and www.biblicalcounselingforwomen.org.

Bruce Roeder

Bruce Roeder is a ACBC\IABC certified biblical counselor and the former ministry partner of Mrs. Julie Ganschow. Together they founded Reigning Grace Counseling Ministries, and coauthored the Process of Biblical Heart Change; the foundation of their biblical counseling and training program at that church.

Today, Bruce serves at Missio Dei Fellowship in Kenosha, Wisconsin as a associateteaching pastor primarily in the area of adult discipleship and biblical counseling.

Bruce holds a Master's Degree in biblical counseling from Master's Divinity School and a B.A. in communication\management from Concordia University as well as an ABS from Moody Bible institute.

Bruce is married to his wonderful wife Liz for more than 40 years. They reside in Kenosha, Wisconsin and have one married son, a sweet daughter-in-law, and three precious grandchildren.

Bruce has a ministry blog titled Church, State, Faith and Culture at http://roedersrants.wordpress.com/

Bruce also writes a History blog titled History Stuff that Interests Me at http://broeder10.wordpress.com/

Made in United States
Troutdale, OR
09/22/2023

13115716R00073